Lewisham and Deptford

A Second Selection

IN OLD PHOTOGRAPHS

Lewisham clock tower, probably decorated for the coronation of Edward VII in August 1902.

Lewisham and Deptford

Deptford

A Second Selection

IN OLD PHOTOGRAPHS

Collected by JOHN COULTER

Alan Sutton Publishing Limited
Phoenix Mill · Thrupp
Stroud · Gloucestershire

First Published 1992

**British Library Cataloguing
in Publication Data**

Coulter, John
Lewisham and Deptford in Old
Photographs: A Second Selection
I. Title
942.163

ISBN 0-7509-0109-8

Typeset in 9/10 Sabon
Typesetting and origination by
Alan Sutton Publishing Limited.
Printed in Great Britain by
WBC Print Ltd, Bridgend.

Contents

For Brian

Or is it just the past? Those flowers, that gate,
These misty parks and motors, lacerate
Simply by being over . . .

Introduction

Despite the ample evidence of experience, we are apt to believe that a second attempt will enable us to make good all the omissions of a first. This was the naive spirit in which I approached my task, but very soon I was faced with the same painful choices as before. In the end it seemed as if quite as many favourite views had found their way on to the rejects pile, and even more treasured facts and anecdotes had fallen to the blue pencil. But this is one of the miseries of authors which is a clear gain to the reader. He is saved from the garrulity of the commentator, and is assured that no makeweights have been introduced among the pictures. Indeed, the wealth of Lewisham's photographic heritage seems as far as ever from being exhausted.

In *Lewisham and Deptford in Old Photographs*, published in 1990, I followed the common practice of arranging views from all parts of the borough in subject groups. This appears to have given satisfaction, so I have adopted the same course for the second selection. But there are changes of detail. The number of sections is reduced from fifteen to twelve. Some of these – 'Rural Fringe' and 'Working Lives', for example – are continued from the first volume, in fact if not in name. Others are completely new: 'Odious Comparisons' traces the history of sites through the use of photographs from different periods, and 'Changed Utterly' illustrates areas which have been obliterated by 1930s slum clearance, by bomb damage, or by post-war redevelopment. The two aerial views in *Lewisham and Deptford in Old Photographs* proved very popular, so this time I have concluded with a section devoted to these fascinating records.

Even more than in the first volume the division into sections is somewhat arbitrary. Most of the views of shops, for example, are gathered together in 'The Purple of Commerce', but others equally good appear in 'Highways', 'Odious Comparisons', and elsewhere. 'Byways' contains pictures that could just as well have fitted into 'Changed Utterly', and vice versa. 'All the Amenities' is a miscellany covering much of the ground of the churches, schools, transport, and public services sections of the first volume; but photographs of relevance to all these subjects will also be found on other pages. The arrangement within sections usually follows some loose pattern: in a number of cases it is a geographical one, from north to south.

As before, the photographs range in date from the 1850s to the 1960s. The stars of the first volume, Henry Wood, Thankfull Sturdee, and William Perkins, are again well represented, and I have found room for more examples of three series which aroused some interest last time: the 1898 pilgrimage down the Ravensbourne, the beautifully detailed interiors of The Hollies, and the antics of the Catford Hill boating enthusiasts.

The photographs of which I have made the least use are views of minor roads. There are large numbers of these available, but except where they are of outstanding quality I have thought that their intense interest to the small number of residents would not compensate for their comparative dullness to the rest. Readers anxious to search for a view of their own street or house, or wishing to pursue any topic connected with the borough's history or topography, should visit the Lewisham Local History Centre, The Manor House, Old Road, Lee, SE13 (telephone 081–852–5050).

I have tried to give the exact location of the scene in each photograph used. After a great deal of map turning – at times it seemed that a resort to table-turning might be the only hope – I think I have succeeded with all but two. These, most annoyingly for a lover of the game, are both cricket scenes: the one at Grove Park on page 111, and the lower picture on page 114. Any information about these would be gratefully received.

What must strike all who glance at these two volumes is how attractive Lewisham was before the First World War, and how ugly today. Of course, this is true to a greater or lesser extent of almost all parts of London – of the country. But Lewisham seems to have suffered to an unusual degree in the loss of objects of beauty, and the acquisition of objects of dismay. There are many culprits, but if a book of photographs can be said to have a villain, then the villain of this one is the motor car. In the best melodramatic tradition it is usually an unseen menace; but for those who know the modern borough well it lurks behind a tree or hedgerow in the most idyllic scenes, ready to spring out in the form of a dual carriageway, a horizontal or vertical car park, a garage or a one-way system. It would not be going too far to say that the invention of the internal combustion engine has been far more terrible in its destructive consequences than the splitting of the atom.

This second selection contains two types of cross references. Those to this volume are identified simply by the page number: for example, 'see p. 105'. But to avoid frequent repetition of a long title, references to the first volume, *Lewisham and Deptford in Old Photographs*, have been given in an abbreviated form. Thus, 'see *I* 105' means 'see '*Lewisham and Deptford in Old Photographs*', p. 105'. Occasionally these two types are combined, as in 'see p. 103 and *I* 151'.

SECTION ONE
Odious Comparisons

Look here upon this picture, and on this . . .

Barclays Bank at Lee Green in 1963 (see p. 11).

The view north along Rushey Green and Lewisham High Street (above, *c*. 1875), from the gate of Rosenthal. This villa, built in the late 1790s, was noted chiefly as the home from *c*. 1830 to 1861 of the flamboyant Alexander Rowland. He was the manufacturer of Macassar Oil, the nineteenth-century Brylcreem, and thus the father of that quintessentially Victorian object, the antimacassar. He once scandalized the congregation at St Mary's church, which is just visible in the distance, by attending service as a walking advertisement for his latest product, with one of his whiskers its native grey and the other dyed a brilliant black. Rosenthal was demolished *c*. 1890, and the photograph below, taken about ten years later, shows how the northern half of the estate was redeveloped. (See also p. 127.) On the right is Rosenthal Road. The house at the corner, No. 41 Rushey Green, was built for a doctor in 1890 and originally called Lulworth. It is now a day centre for children. Note how it inherited some trees from the garden of Rosenthal.

Eltham Road seen from Lee Green, c. 1870, with Burnt Ash Road on the right. Lee Green Farm occupied this corner until the 1860s. Orchard Terrace, the row of shops in the foreground, was built on a piece of spare land in 1863–64, and Eastbourne Terrace, beyond, on the site of the farmhouse, c. 1869. (See p. 15 for further views of Eastbourne Terrace.) H.F. Cockle was the second tenant of the corner shop. He began in 1869 as an oil and colour man, like several of his family in Lewisham and Deptford, but by 1874 had become principally a grocer. He later took over the adjoining shop – Miss Collins's Berlin wool depository in 1870 – and continued trading until 1898. The third shop, with the garden rollers outside, was that of John Aldous, ironmonger. On the opposite side of the road can be glimpsed the entrance to a small beershop, run by Henry Lippard in 1870, on the site now occupied by the Help the Blind shop. Cockle's corner was taken over in 1902 by the London and Provincial Bank, which became part of Barclays (see p. 9). It was demolished in 1967, when all of these shops gave place to Leegate House and the Leegate shopping centre.

The part of Lewisham High Street opposite St Mary's churchyard has a long history, and several old buildings survive there. Among them are the semi-detached pair on the left above, which were built in 1791 and are now part of Olby's premises. The allegedly Elizabethan properties on the right were demolished shortly after this photograph was taken, *c.* 1875. They were called Pilcher's Cottages after Thomas Pilcher, the builder and estate agent who lived in the house in the *c.* 1857 photograph below. This was demolished in 1906, but the seventeenth-century building behind the tree, which was the shop of the Ingersoll dynasty of vets for eighty years from the 1830s, is still standing as Nos 315 and 317.

Ingersoll's shop reappears as Infirmary House in the 1880s view above. The whitewashed building to the right of the Congregational church spire was Streete House, now the Hire Shop. The tall group in the centre was built in the late 1870s on part of the site of Pilcher's Cottages (top left). Next to Infirmary House was the Coach and Horses, an old pub which went dry for a century before being re-founded in the 1860s. The little shop on the extreme right was formerly the shed for the parish fire engine. By the late 1920s (below) it had been displaced by Romborough Way (see *I 34*), and Streete House had become a shop. The tall block in the middle was built in 1906–07, on the site of Pilcher's house. Olby's main building has now replaced it.

John Addey, Master Shipwright at Deptford Dockyard, who died in 1606, left money to the poor of the town. In 1820 the Charity Commissioners decided that the old haphazard distribution was unsatisfactory, and directed that the money should be used for educating poor children. Addey's School in Church Street was built in 1821, and enlarged in 1861–2. The photograph above shows it in 1956. In the 1880s and '90s Addey's was combined with other Deptford charities (notably Stanhope's, see *I 92*) to form the Addey and Stanhope School. The Addey building was used until the present school in New Cross Road (below) was ready in 1899. The old school was adapted to various uses, notably as a laundry and factory, before it was demolished in the early 1970s.

The shops of Eastbourne Terrace, Eltham Road (see p. 11) were gradually acquired in the late nineteenth century by the firm of Reed and Co., and built up into a department store which stretched across Carston Mews into Orchard Terrace. In 1902, shortly before the date of the photograph above, the name changed to Griffith and Co., but the store only survived until 1913. It was thus standing conveniently idle in 1914, when the Army Service Corps took over the Greenwich Workhouse, later Grove Park Hospital, and began scouring the district for billets. Several ASC men appear in the photograph below, taken at Christmas 1916. Carston Mews was one of the countless local stables of Thomas Tilling (see I 84). This whole area was cleared in 1967 for the Leegate Centre.

The Old House, Sydenham, which stood until 1899 or 1900 on a site now between Sydenham Road and Earlsthorpe Road, was probably built *c*. 1713 for Edward Hodsdon, a wine merchant; but it was principally associated with the family of Mayow, the owners from 1787 until the house was sold to a developer. The last of them to live in the Old House was Mayow Wynell Adams (1808–98), whose mother was a Mayow. He was born and died at the Old House, spent most of his life in Sydenham, and came to be regarded as the village squire and patriarch. Until Adams sold the site for Mayow Park (see p. 114) at a knock-down price in 1877, his grounds ran north from Sydenham Road to Perry Vale. He was always ready to throw them open for garden parties, Sunday school treats, and the like. In this photograph the youth of Sydenham are seen enjoying a game of football in the Old House grounds. Their pitch now lies beneath the 'Thorpe' estate (see opposite).

The Old House estate was bought from Mayow Adams's heirs by the building firm of Edmondson and Son. The house was demolished, and in 1900 a long parade of shops was built on the Sydenham Road frontage. The view above, taken *c.* 1907, shows the western end of the parade, from the corner of Queensthorpe Road. This survives little altered, but the section between Queensthorpe and Mayow Roads was partially destroyed during the Second World War. On the garden of the Old House Edmondson and Son began to build the Thorpe roads – Earlsthorpe, Kingsthorpe, etc. – in 1901. Queensthorpe Road (below, *c.* 1910) was one of the first to be completed. The view is northwards towards Bishopsthorpe Road, and shows the valley which appears in the photograph of the Old House opposite.

Rushey Green in 1897, looking south from Brownhill Road. The indistinct building in the distance is the Old Black Horse (see *I* 59) just before demolition; one of the large pair of houses in the centre was the former Catford police station (see *I* 112). This, and the larger group of weather-boarded cottages were demolished *c.* 1905 to make way for Bank Buildings. The premises of W.F. Power, the framer and gilder, and B. Weatherley and Sons, the cycle agents, (formerly a wheelwright's forge) survived until 1913, when the Queen's Hall cinema, later the Gaumont (seen on the right in the lower photograph opposite) replaced them. The Lewisham Hippodrome, later the Eros cinema, was built in 1911 on the site of two large houses: Crookwood, which stood at the corner of Brownhill Road, and Umberslade, which lay behind Weatherley's. The Gaumont and Eros were closed in 1959, and demolished in 1960. The corner is now occupied by Eros House, a tower block so hideous that it won a Civic Trust architectural award in 1964. Through all these changes the old pump has survived, and remains an unexpected embellishment of Rushey Green.

Michael Whitehall was an old bachelor with a passion for the perpetuation of his name. In 1888 he gave a stained-glass window to Prendergast School (see *I* 96), and in his will contributed heavily to the expense of the clock tower; but the great bid for immortality was the Whitehall Memorial Fountain, which was erected between the town hall and St Laurence's church (above) in 1898. Almost at once it became a nuisance, obstructing traffic and tripping unwary pedestrians on dark nights. In 1920 the council persuaded Whitehall's trustees to let it be moved to a new site in front of the Lewisham Hippodrome, at the corner of Brownhill Road (below, in the late 1920s). It was apparently still there in 1950, but by 1959 it had gone, I know not whither. Alas, poor Whitehall!

The view from Catford Road towards the town hall and Rushey Green (above, *c.* 1910). On the left is the garden of Elmwood (see pp. 156–7), and beyond it the entrance to Springfield Park Crescent, now Catford Broadway. The trees in the centre hide Hatcliffe's almshouses, which were built in 1857 and removed in 1925, when the shops known as the Catford Arcade, seen below, were built on the site. They lasted until 1961, when the irresistible growth of the new town hall demanded their demolition. Norman's sold, emphatically, not dresses but gowns, the distinction being (as I can reveal on the best feminine authority) that a gown is more dressy.

SECTION TWO

Highways

With carts, and cars, and coaches roaring all:
Wide-poured abroad, behold the prowling crew;
See how they dash along from wall to wall!

Lewisham High Street, *c.* 1910, showing part of the site of the modern street market.

Evelyn Street, the old lower road linking Deptford with London, used to be graced with long terraces of good quality eighteenth- and early nineteenth-century houses, now almost all demolished. Some of the side turnings have also perished: Hood Street, on the left in this view of *c.* 1905, has dwindled into a mere footpath. The Black Horse survives, though, as does Gosterwood Street on the right. Above the horse tram are St Luke's church, and Deptford fire station, which was rebuilt in this form in 1903.

Deptford High Street, looking north towards the railway bridge, *c.* 1911. The turning on the right, by the Prince Regent, is Frankham Street, formerly known as Regent Street. This card was sent to her sister by one Bessie Town, with the advice (which I pass on for what it is worth): 'There may be other chaps quite winning, sweet, and gay; But always choose the chap with dancing eyes of grey.'

But for the saving grace of the milk cart, this 1907 view might be entitled 'the teetotaller's nightmare'. We are looking from Lewisham High Road (now Way) into New Cross Road. On the right is the Marquis of Granby; behind its lamp is the large wine merchant's shop (later the site of the Kinema, see I 127), then run by G.H. Robinson, the landlord of the New Cross Inn, which appears above the tram. And on the left is the golden cross sign of the New Cross House, now the Goldsmiths' Tavern.

The slummy or Greenwich end of Lewisham Road contrasted sharply with the smart southern half (see p. 75). This photograph of c. 1909 shows the view northwards, with the corner of Orchard Hill on the left. To the right of the tram, and behind the sign of the Ordnance Arms, is the bridge over the Greenwich Park branch railway (see I 30 and 31), just above the platform of Blackheath Hill station. In the distance is part of John Penn and Sons' works (see p. 103 and I 151) at the corner of John Penn Street.

The junction of Brockley Road and Brockley Grove, the turning to the right, *c.* 1918. These were two ancient lanes linking Deptford and Lewisham with the hamlet of Brockley and with Sydenham Common. 'Brockley' covered a large district on either side of the Deptford and Lewisham boundary, but the hamlet was in the area now usually known as Crofton Park – a change resulting from one of the accidents of railway history. The pair of houses at the junction were called Joy Cottages, and later St Germans Cottages after the owner, the Earl of St Germans. They were built *c.* 1860 on the site of a barn belonging to Brockley Green Farm (see *I* 12), and demolished in the 1930s. The shops numbered 397 to 407 Brockley Road now occupy the site. There was an attractive little green in front of the cottages; the march of progress has turned it into a traffic island graced with a public convenience.

Deptford Broadway, looking east towards Church Street and the bridge, *c.* 1910. The Scotch House was built for Gardiner and Co., tailors and outfitters, in 1882–3, and they traded here until the late 1950s. The many houses and shops cleared to create the site included two old Deptford Bridge pubs, the Mitre and the Feathers. This important corner is now far less memorably occupied by an anonymous red brick office block. J. and H. Robinson's Deptford Bridge Mills, behind, were largely destroyed by fire in 1970.

This view up Blackheath Hill, *c.* 1910, misrepresents Holy Trinity church (which was sadly destroyed in the Second World War) because one of its distinctive twin spires is hiding the other. On the right is the Horse and Groom, rebuilt in 1937, of which John Baggerley was the landlord for many years until 1912. That was also the year in which the attractive houses on the left were demolished. Cade Tyler House now occupies the site.

Lewisham High Road, now Lewisham Way, looking north-west from Manor Road. This postcard shows clearly the valley of the stream which used to run between Rokeby Road and Malpas Road. The shop on the left, at the corner of Upper Brockley Road (No. 158, then and now a newsagents) is advertising *John Bull*, a magazine started in 1906; but the date of this card is probably *c.* 1914. John Tyson, the cheesemonger at No. 185, closed down in 1915.

The Memorial Gardens in Lewisham Way, seen here in the 1930s, were laid out as a private amenity for the residents of Wickham Terrace (the crescent behind, which was built between 1849 and 1855) and bought by Deptford Council in 1924. This view from Breakspears Road shows Brockley Congregational church (see p. 124) and, on the left, the part of Wickham Terrace destroyed in 1959 to make way for the Wickham Building of Lewisham College – a very poor exchange. One of these houses (No. 196) was the home of the great Marie Lloyd in 1891–2.

Lewisham High Street in the late 1920s, seen from the tower of the Salisbury, a pub demolished in 1959. This picture illustrates the then intense competition between Lewisham's department stores, now reduced to a single survivor. Sayers the chemist, on the far left, was acquired *c*. 1930 by the Chiesman Brothers (now the Army and Navy), who built their staircase bay here. Stroud's store, which had long struggled with the Chiesmans for supremacy on the High Pavement, was taken over by the Royal Arsenal Co-Operative Society, *c*. 1926. In 1933 they were to build Tower House (see p. 85) on the site. In the centre of the picture is Dubois's department store (see p. 78) at the corner of Lewis Grove, subsequently replaced by a number of small shops. Amidst all this change, the two banks on the right, the Midland built *c*. 1898, and Barclays of *c*. 1880, have so far been bastions of comforting continuity.

Loampit Vale, *c.* 1908, looking west towards the railway bridge built for the Tonbridge line of the South Eastern Railway, which opened in 1865. Almost all the old houses east of the bridge have been demolished, including the Hope public house, seen here on the left. The exceptions to this wholesale destruction are the shops on the right, built in the 1860s, which are now Nos 66 to 76.

Lewisham High Street, south from the corner of Rennell Street, in the 1870s. The first four shops, built in the late 1850s as Sundridge Terrace, still survive somewhat altered. At this time they were occupied by William Powell, butcher, Isaac Short, grocer (it is his cart outside), Frederick Burton, watchmaker, and W.J. Clement, hairdresser. The next shop was later to become Lonsdale and Bradey (see p. 95). Above the horse's head can be seen the original premises of the Joiners Arms. The pub was rebuilt in its present form *c.* 1908.

The junction of Lewisham High Street and Loampit Vale was known as The Obelisk, after the drinking fountain seen on the left below. The southern corner of the two roads was occupied from the late 1880s by Obelisk Buildings (on the left above). Sainsbury's established one of their provision shops there c. 1891, and when the neighbouring drapery store closed down Sainsbury's took it over as an experiment. They persisted until c. 1930, and then wisely withdrew to the certain profits of food. The photograph above shows Sainsbury's drapery in 1907, with Tucker's drug store (see I 135) beyond. By the early 1920s (below) Sainsbury's had extended considerably, but this new section was pulled down c. 1931 to make way for the Gaumont cinema (see I 127). The shops beyond were demolished last year; the successor to the Duke of Cambridge, on the right, survived until 1992.

Here is a photograph to break the motorist's heart. It shows the central section of Lewisham High Street, at its notorious junction with Ladywell Road (the turning to the left) as it was *c.* 1874, without even a flock of sheep to clutter the road. All the buildings on the right, south of Lewisham Congregational (now United Reformed) church, have since been swept away to build the Ladywell Baths, or Leisure Centre, in 1965, and the fire station in 1968. Friend Westover opened his grocery shop, on the right, in the 1840s, and the family stayed until 1891. Afterwards it was for many years the premises of John Balsdon, the butcher. The first house beyond the church, on the southern corner of Courthill Road, was built *c.* 1871. It was a wine merchant's in its early years and later the local Conservative Party headquarters. Beyond is the old house called Yew Tree Villa (see p. 128). The spire above its roof will probably puzzle all but veteran residents. It belonged to the Lewisham Wesleyan church in Albion Road (now Way) which was built in 1870 and destroyed by bombing during the Second World War. (It appears in the aerial photograph on pp. 150 and 151). Compare this picture with the top one on p. 13, which it continues northwards.

This photograph of Lewisham High Street was taken in the early 1880s, at the same time as those of the Castle and Lewisham House (see *I* 58 and 43), and contains some of the same extras. The point of view is just south of the Castle. The shops were those of Charles Reed, chemist, E.H. Lashbrook, stationer and post master, and James Tait, baker. The tall building beyond was the Black Bull, now, alas, the Fox and Firkin.

If the photographer were still standing in the same position 120 years later, he would be well placed – barring stiffness – to catch a bus opposite Lewisham Hospital. The buildings shown are the edge of the eighteenth-century house called The Jasmines; a terrace called Grove Place, built *c.* 1870 on the site of Cole's lunatic asylum and bombed with The Jasmines in 1944; Colfe's almshouses of 1664, also bombed, and demolished in 1958 to make way for the register office; Cliff Villa and Sion House, the site of Lewisham Library; and St Mary's church.

The sylvan charm of the Victorian Lee High Road is illustrated by these two photographs of the 1880s. Both look towards the Rose of Lee, and both have the garden of Hurst Lodge (see p. 99) on the right. The view above was taken from the corner of Belgrave Villas, now Glenton Road. Woodland Cottage, on the left, was demolished *c.* 1905, so that Lee's architecture could be enriched by the lock-up garages at the corner of Rembrandt Road. The two houses between Manor Park and Weardale Road, below, were originally called Clifton Villa and Manor Villa. The former has now been enlarged as flats, but Manor Villa, always a doctor's house, is little altered. The Rose of Lee was founded in 1859 and rebuilt in its present form *c.* 1897.

Parasols were at a premium when this view of Lee Green was taken between 1900 and 1905. Tilling's horse buses would now find the road a little crowded, but in other respects the scene is not much changed today. The Old Tiger's Head (left) had been rebuilt in 1896, and the New Tiger's Head a few years later. Kent House, at the bottom of Lee Road, was one of the branches of Austin and Co. before their merger with Cave and Son c. 1898 (see *I* 137). It is now a video store. Another of the shops in this terrace became the local Barclays Bank when the one at the corner of Eltham Road (see p. 9) was demolished. The main change is that the site of the present post office, between the New Tiger and Osborn Terrace, was then occupied by small shops similar to the ones still surviving on the Eltham Road side of the pub. (Originally the terrace had been continuous, and the New Tiger was probably founded in a cottage like these.) The shops, behind the stationary bus, were then occupied by James Basil Bell, an estate agent, and by Sydney Lycett and Co., engineers.

The point where Rushey Green becomes Lewisham High Street, seen here in the 1870s, with St Mary's church in the distance. George Lane turns off to the right, with the George Inn (see *I* 82) at the corner. The garden wall beyond belonged to The Maples (see p. 102). The building glimpsed behind the George sign and the flagpole was the end house of Mount Pleasant Place, a pair of terraces built on either side of Mount Pleasant Road in the early 1870s. It is now a shop numbered 377 Lewisham High Street. The group on the right was known as Navy Place. The pair of substantial brick houses, later Nos 7 and 9 Rushey Green, were built in 1744. The far one, No. 7, was the home in the 1880s of Michael Whitehall (see p. 19). The wooden cottages on either side were probably added *c*. 1770. The site of Navy Place is now occupied by the Department of Health and Social Security office, perhaps the least interesting building in Lewisham. For all its bulk, I must have passed it a hundred times before I noticed it was there.

Two views of Rushey Green, *c.* 1908, both showing the spire of the Catford Methodist church (see p. 127). The one above looks north from Brownhill Road, at a time when there were still mostly houses behind the greens on the east side, and the shops were largely confined to the west. Two pubs are featured. Beside the tram is the sign of the Rising Sun, which still survives in its 1937 rebuilding. On the left, above Nevill's van, is a far less familiar watering hole, the Gothic Cottage beershop, which had closed by 1910. The photograph below shows the scene north from Wildfell Road. The corner shop was the Maypole Dairy. The tall building with the washing hanging from the window was the off-licence of the Plough and Harrow (see I 59).

The southern end of Rushey Green, *c.* 1910, showing two Catford branches of Barclays Bank. On the right is No. 191, then the London and South Western, later Barclays, now a travel agency. The whitewashed building on the left is No. 166, the London and Provincial in 1910 and the current Barclays. The Black Horse (see *I* 59) is in the centre, and an early Catford Sainsbury's at No. 193 on the right.

Brownhill Road originated in the late 1870s as a short cul-de-sac off Rushey Green. Its projectors had no greater ambitions for it than the developers of Rosenthal and Ringstead Roads for their creations. The change came in the 1890s, with the building of the Corbett Estate (see p. 148), which extended Brownhill to its chance meeting with St Mildred's Road, and a future as a major highway. This view of *c.* 1905 looks towards Rushey Green and shows the Baptist church (built 1903) on the left, and the Brownhill Market, later called The Pavement, on the right.

SECTION THREE

Rural Fringe

Let us, as by this verdant bank we float,
Search down the marge to find some shady pool
Where we may rest a while and moor our boat
And bathe our tired limbs in the waters cool.

A field near Southend Village, *c*. 1910.

Deptford and New Cross were once celebrated for their market gardens, but they were gradually built over until the only survivor was Stephen Smith's in Evelyn Street, seen here in the 1920s. It was a triangular piece of land, between the present Croft Street and Rainsborough Avenue. The London County Council bought it in the early 1930s, and built Hazlewood House and Pomona House there, the latter gracefully, or tastelessly, according to your point of view, recalling John Evelyn's classic treatise on cider.

The old Brockley Jack (see *I 54*) was a favourite subject for the camera. This is the present, less photogenic building which replaced it in 1898. The real point of interest in the view is the farmhouse of College Farm, which survived until *c.* 1913, although its fields had been built over long before. Nos 414 to 418 Brockley Road are now on the site of the house. College Farm was so called because it belonged to Christ's Hospital, the school of Coleridge and Lamb.

Until this century these were the only two houses in the part of Ladywell Road west of the Ladywell Tavern. Bridge House Farm (above) belonged to the trust – a branch of the Corporation of London – responsible for the upkeep of London Bridge, and later of the other Thames crossings. In 1897, when these photographs were taken, it was called Dutton's Farm, after William Leslie Dutton, the tenant. The site of the farmhouse is now occupied by the northern end of Chudleigh Road. The Ladywell mineral spring cottage (below) stood on a spot now covered by No. 148 Ladywell Road, which bears a commemorative plaque. The tenants of the cottage sold supposedly therapeutic water from a well in the garden. It was a poor man's Epsom, or perhaps even a beggar's Sydenham. Both farm and cottage were demolished c. 1899.

I expressed regret in the first selection at not having room for all of the series of photographs recording an 1898 trip down the Ravensbourne. These two and the top picture opposite are further examples, and there is one more on p. 116. The notice being treated with such obvious awe – for did not Victorian children respect authority? – was at Bellingham Farm (see *I* 15), which can just be seen in the background. The two- and four-footed paddlers, below, were in 'Catford Rec', otherwise Ladywell Fields.

Few gudgeon, I imagine, now flourish in the River Ravensbourne, but in 1898 this reach on the north side of Catford Bridge was known as 'the Gudgeon Swim'. Carpers may think this was over-optimistic even then, given that the Pool River, which passes through the grounds of the Bell Green gasworks, falls into the Ravensbourne above this point.

To capture this apparently rustic scene the photographer had to stand under the railway viaduct where it crosses the Ravensbourne east of Catford Hill. The landing stage in the background was that of Clovelly, No. 33 Catford Hill (see *I 25*). The sluice controlled the supply of water to the race of Catford Bridge Mill.

A soldier and his girl stroll amid the pastoral charms of Bromley Road during the First World War, while a Tilling country bus makes its way to Southend Village. This is the part of the original highway now bypassed and known as Old Bromley Road (see also p. 43). The view is south-eastwards from the bend towards what it is now the junction with the new part of Bromley Road, Ashgrove Road and Bromley Hill. The buildings to the right of the bus, then the only houses in Ashgrove Road, are now Nos. 10 and 12. On the far right is the roof of one of the pavilions serving the Spartan Athletic ground.

The yard of Shroffold's Farm (see *I* 16) *c.* 1910, when the farmer was George Candy. The three women teasing the dogs were (left to right) his wife Charlotte, and his daughters Ruby and Blanche.

Meadow Cottages, Southend, photographed c. 1910. They belonged to the Cator family, and were leased with the Upper Mill (see p. 44), which was also a farm. The cottages stood a few hundred yards south of the mill, on the present Old Bromley Road (see p. 42). They were demolished *c.* 1925, and No. 15 Old Bromley Road is now on the site.

The Upper Mill at Southend Village was probably established before the Norman Conquest. Here it is seen from the south-east, *c.* 1860, when William Turner Kelsey was the miller. The mill pond was later transformed into watercress beds, and is now the site of Bamford and Chelford Roads. The buildings, which were last used by a timber merchant, were demolished in the late 1960s.

The Lower Mill at Southend, probably also of pre-Conquest origin, stood just south of the Tiger's Head (see p. 68). The mill pond, seen here *c.* 1905, later became a boating lake called Peter Pan's Pool, and is now the Homebase Pool. On the far left is Southend Hall, the home of the Forster family, demolished in 1937; in the centre, the St John's Schools, which survived until 1983; and on the right, the houses, themselves no longer extant, which replaced Mott's cottage and others (see I 49). Southend chapel, behind the carriage, is happily still standing.

The view from Bellingham Farm towards Bromley Road in 1927, five or six years before Waterbank Road was built on this field. It was called 'Waterbank' because the River Ravensbourne flows, invisibly, across this scene, between the camera and the road. Comparison with the photograph of the farm on I 15, which is almost the reverse of this one, makes the point clear. The bus is travelling northwards from Southend Village to Catford past the wall of Park House, the old manor house of Bellingham, which was destroyed by bombing in 1944. The open space to the left of the wall was the United Dairies Sports Club cricket ground, of which the pavilion is just masked by the chestnut. In the distance are the remaining fields of Whitehouse Farm. These fields, the cricket ground, and the gardens of Park House are now covered by Conisborough Crescent, etc.

Durham Farm, Grove Park, was something of an upstart compared with Claypit Farm, which stood opposite. It was only established, and the farmhouse built, in the 1840s. Its dairy herds grazed the fields on the north-eastern side of Marvels Lane, an area now largely occupied by sports grounds. The farmhouse, which was situated about half-way between Grove Park Road and the hospital, was demolished *c.* 1923, and the site is now occupied by Nos. 97 and 99 Marvels Lane. The photograph was taken *c.* 1910, when Ernest Adams was the farmer. It shows two of the carts which he used for his milk delivery service.

Spicer's Cottage stood at the turn of Marvels Lane, next to Grove Park Hospital, and just over 100 yd east of the library. It was sometimes ridiculously called 'the smuggler's cottage' (smuggling what, from where?), but was really occupied by labourers of Lee Green Farm. The 1720 date on the building seems quite plausible. It was demolished *c.* 1912.

Holloway Farm was one of several which lost their fields to the Downham Estate in the 1920s. It is seen here *c.* 1897, when Daniel Dutton was the farmer. He was the last, remaining until the house was demolished in the late '20s. The site of the farmyard is now covered by houses in Kendale Road and Beechmont Close.

Sydenham Common was made available for building purposes by the Lewisham Enclosure Act of 1810, but much of the higher ground towards Sydenham Hill became farmland instead, and was only gradually nibbled by the developers in the late nineteenth century. This extensive view was taken in the 1880s from the Hillcrest Road area, off Westwood Hill, and looks towards Sydenham Hill and the upper reaches of Wells Park Road. On the right is the curve of Longton Avenue, before any houses were built on the western side. The large building in the distance, above Longton Avenue, was the booking hall of Upper Sydenham station, on the Crystal Palace and South London Junction Railway. The station, which opened in 1884 and closed in 1954, is now divided into flats numbered 151 to 159 Wells Park Road. High Level Drive has bulldozed through the blackberry bushes in the foreground, and the Hillcrest Estate has evicted the cows from the field in the middle distance.

SECTION FOUR

Working Lives

And for them many a weary hand did swelt
In torched mines and noisy factories . . .

The men, and boys, of Sydenham police station, Dartmouth Road (see *I* 112), *c.* 1870.

The old mast pond, where masts were floated for weathering, at the Royal Victoria Yard, Deptford (see *I* 106). It was later used as a dock, and the site is now the southern part of Pepys Park. Behind the schooner is one of the engines of the yard's own narrow gauge railway.

The Royal Victoria Yard was largely rebuilt in the 1780s to the designs of James Arrow, Surveyor to the Victualling Office. A few examples of his work survive, converted into flats on the Pepys Estate. Among them are the houses known as the Colonnade (seen above, *c.* 1900), which were occupied by the Porter and the Clerk of Cheque. The fine gateway, leading out to Grove Street, is also by Arrow.

The great Thames flood of 7 January 1928 killed many people in the Westminster area. In Deptford the loss was only of property, but this was serious, especially in and around the Royal Victoria Yard. The 17 ft outer wall collapsed in a section 180 ft long opposite the modern Dragoon Road. In the top left corner of this photograph are the backs of houses in Grove Street (see *I* 115) which suffered severe damage as a result of the breaching of this wall.

Brockley Hall was built late in the eighteenth century, on the site of an ancient farmhouse. It occupied some thirteen acres in the southern angle of Brockley Grove and Brockley Road, part of it garden and part farmland (see *I* 18). The owners from the 1840s until the house was demolished in 1932, and Brockley Hall Road built in its place, were the Noakes family. They were the proprietors of a brewery at Bermondsey, taken over by John Courage in 1930, and their ales were sold at a number of local pubs, including the Brockley Jack. This is the gate lodge, the site of which is now occupied by Nos 24 to 28 Brockley Grove. The photograph was probably taken in the early 1890s, and if so shows the Noakes's gardener John Osmond, with his wife Emily and one of their daughters.

The Boys' Industrial Home at Shaftesbury House, Perry Rise, *c.* 1910. These Forest Hill homes, for orphaned or neglected children, had been founded in Rojack Road: for boys in 1873, and for girls in 1881, when the great Earl of Shaftesbury made a speech. The boys moved to Perry Rise in 1883, and the girls to Louise House in Dartmouth Road in 1891. For some reason all the boys were taught shoemaking, which must have become a drug on the labour market. Shaftesbury House is now one of Lewisham Council's day centres for children.

The St Olave's Union workhouse, later known as Ladywell Lodge (see *I 52*) in 1917, when it was serving as a military hospital. The block shown here is the nearest one, just above the Roman Catholic chapel, in the aerial view on p. 159.

Two flour carts from Robinson's Deptford Bridge mills in Springfield Park Crescent, Catford, *c*. 1905. They are outside the back door of Lewisham town hall, part of the extension built in 1900. Beyond it is the council yard (see the top picture opposite), and in the distance the London and Provincial bank, now Barclays, in Rushey Green. Springfield Park Crescent was created – roughly on the line of a straight footpath – in 1867, and given its modern name of Catford Broadway in 1939.

Laying tram lines in Lee High Road during the winter of 1906/7. The scene is perhaps between Dacre Park and Boone Street, as the spectator in the plain apron is the blacksmith Stephen Hollett (see *I* 104), whose forge was in Dacre Park.

The workmen of the brand new Lewisham Metropolitan Borough Council pose for their portrait in the town hall yard in 1900. If they look jaded, it is because they had only just stopped fulfilling the same role for the tired old Lewisham Board of Works. The yard existed from *c.* 1874 until 1932, when it became the site of the town hall extension and concert hall, now the Lewisham Theatre (see *I* 144–5).

Jealous on hearing that Deptford Council had two motorized dust carts, Lewisham's Works and Highways Committee decided in 1923 to order one for themselves. It was known as the 'S.D. Freighter', and was made by Shelvoke and Drewry of Letchworth. After a series of trials against the horse carts, the freighter showed a sensational saving of $3\frac{1}{2}d$. per ton of refuse collected, and a second vehicle was ordered immediately. The first is here shown on parade at the new Bellingham Estate.

The industrial town of Deptford gave solid support to the General Strike of May 1926. A key battleground in the local struggle was the New Cross tram depot (see *I* 87), which was vital to London's transport system. This photograph shows one of the special cars, manned by strike-breaking volunteers, as the police prepare to escort it from the depot.

The aristocratic committee which controlled the Deptford Fund (see *I* 142) became alarmed during the 1930s by the high rate of unemployment in the area, which made it 'a struggle to get the boys interested in anything but Communism'. Their response was to start keep-fit classes at the Albany Institute (since demolished) in Creek Road. This 1936 photograph shows the instructor, Mr Spanton, on the left.

New Cross Hospital was opened in 1877 as the Deptford Hospital for pauper smallpox patients during the epidemic of that year. The wooden buildings were intended only as a temporary emergency measure, but recurring epidemics kept the hospital in use. Between 1904 and 1906, known by now as the South Eastern, it was rebuilt in a more solid form. Part remains in medical use, as the New Cross Day Hospital, etc., but most has been demolished, and is now the site of Avonley Village. This nurse and ambulance were probably photographed c. 1906.

Men of the 26th Motor Ambulance Convoy of the Royal Army Medical Corps photographed in Catford in 1916, shortly before they were posted overseas.

King and Sons began business *c*. 1905 in Wagner Street off the Old Kent Road, as poultry feed and dog biscuit manufacturers. During the First World War they won valuable contracts to supply the services, and moved to larger premises in Staplehurst Road, next to Hither Green station. Their new headquarters had been built in 1913 as the Globe cinema, an enterprise which had never prospered. It was while at Hither Green that King and Sons adopted the name Chiltonian for the business, in honour of the founder's wife, who had been a Miss Chilton. They now moved into the growing market for human biscuits, with such success that in 1924 they were able to start building their 'model factory' in Manor Lane, Lee, on part of the site of the Granville Cricket Club ground (see p. 112). The whole operation had been transferred to Lee by 1930. The photograph above shows the packing room at Staplehurst Road, *c*. 1918, when the pressures of war meant that the workforce was predominantly female. The old Hither Green factory still survives; it is now the Wolseley Drainage Centre.

The Chiltonian factory in Manor Lane, Lee, in the early 1930s. The photograph above shows the transport fleet in the forecourt. The railway embankment between Hither Green and Lee can be seen in the background. Below is the laboratory. I cannot make up my mind whether the biscuits were the objects of experimentation, or a perk of the job. The firm was absorbed by Allied Biscuits in the 1970s, and the factory was closed in 1980 and soon demolished. The Chiltonian Industrial Estate has taken its place.

One of the milk carts of the Hope Farm Dairy in 1912, when the proprietor was William Winkworth. The business, formerly known as the Grove Park Dairy Company, had its headquarters at No. 2 Heather Road, but the cows are said to have been kept in the fields at the turn of Marvels Lane, between the library and the hospital.

A flower seller at Lee Green in the 1920s. The view is from Barclays Bank, at the corner of Burnt Ash Road and Eltham Road (see p. 9), towards the side windows of Dennis's butcher's shop in Lee High Road. The drinking fountain had been removed by 1949.

SECTION FIVE

Pleasures of the People

But on Sunday we slip our tether,
And away from the smoke and the smirch;
Too grateful to God for his Sabbath
To shut its hours in a church.

The new Prince of Wales Picture Playhouse in Lewisham High Street (see *I* 126) in October 1922.

Bonfires were a popular way of celebrating national, and especially royal events. They were frequently planned as chains of beacons stretching across the country, each giving the signal for the lighting of the next; but more often than not mist or rain would intervene to disrupt the process. Hilly Fields is obviously an ideal spot for the purpose, and shortly after the park was opened it was chosen as the site for the Deptford bonfire to mark Queen Victoria's Golden Jubilee on 22 June 1887. Ten thousand spectators were present. Thankfull Sturdee's photograph shows the preparation of the bonfire, constructed largely of railway sleepers and tar barrels, which reached a height of forty feet.

Blackheath was another fine site for bonfires. The one above, built for the Diamond Jubilee on 22 June 1897, was lit by Edward Stidolph of Langdale House, No. 136 Greenwich Road, while the boys from the Montague House Orphanage in Dartmouth Hill 'sang lustily *God Save the Queen*'. The Hilly Fields bonfire for the coronation of King George V on 22 June 1911 (below) was paid for by the LCC, and it was the head park keeper, Mr W. Bashford, who applied the match. The photograph shows the band-stand (see p. 70), and on the right the tower of St Peter's church in Wickham Road.

CORONATION BONFIRE BROCKLEY. JUNE 22ND 1911.

Almost every street in Deptford was roped off to celebrate King George V's Silver Jubilee in May 1935 with a riotous party. This was Ffinch Street, built as Seymour Street in the 1840s, but renamed in 1886 in memory of a rector of St Paul's. It used to be a cul-de-sac, running from the High Street to the railway viaduct; a platform of Deptford station can be seen in the background. All the houses were demolished in the 1960s, and their place is now largely devoted to car parking.

The first tram from Lee Green to Lewisham passing The Woodman public house in Lee High Road (which was rebuilt in this form in 1887) on 4 May 1907. Was the man on the bike clearing the way with a whistle? Street spectacles were always sure to attract a crowd; but this one seems to have been more interested in the photographer than the tram.

The Blackheath bank holiday funfairs (see *I* 120) were, of course, especially popular with children, as these two postcards of *c.* 1905 illustrate. The scene above is in the angle of Shooters Hill Road and Duke Humphrey Road, with Greenwich Park in the background. The two girls on the left are descending into the Old Donkey Pit, at one period a place where donkeys for hire were tethered but probably disused by this time. It has long since been filled in. A popular free amusement was provided by the ponds on the heath. The Whitefield Pond near Whitefield's Mount (below) had practically dried up even before the recent drought.

A bicycle club outing about to start from Dacre Street, Lee, probably at the height of the cycling boom, *c.* 1896, when H.G. Wells's *The Wheels of Chance* was a best seller. For Dacre Street, now called Fludyer Street, see p. 82.

Catford-Southend Football Club, known more familiarly as the Kittens or the Enders, played in Bromley Road, apparently in front of Robertson's jam factory (see p. 158) until 1912, when they moved to a new ground in Mountsfield Park (see I 150). They came to grief when, after incurring great expense in improving the ground, their merger with Charlton Athletic in 1922/3 failed to last. This card was sent to his girlfriend by 'the tramp-like individual in plain clothes on the right', during the 1907/8 season.

The curriculum at Brockley Road School certainly appears to have been eccentric, if truly represented by these volumes (see *I* 97). Maypole dancing was part of the educational authorities' desire to interest children in the traditional sports and customs of the people. (Tug-of-war, below, fell into the same category.) The trees beyond the playground were across the road in the Roman Catholic section of Brockley Cemetery.

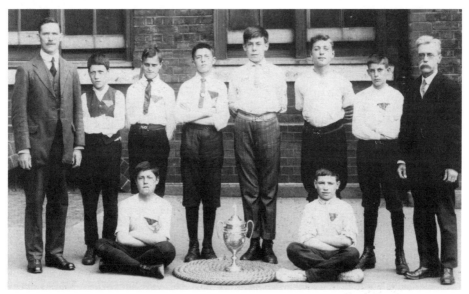

These tug-of-war champions of 1920 were from Lucas Street School in Deptford New Town. This had begun as the Tanners Hill Infant School in 1840, and after several rebuildings and repositionings, is now Lucas Vale School in Thornville Street.

The Two Brewers in Perry Hill (see *I* 60) is shown above *c.* 1860, when the landlord was George Sykes. Below is the Tiger's Head in Bromley Road, Southend, which probably began its chequered career early in the eighteenth century as The George. The Tiger's Head was rebuilt *c.* 1905, but then entirely destroyed by a flying bomb in July 1944. Eighteen people were killed. The site lay derelict until 1958, when the present pub was built. It was known for a time as The Squire, but has happily reverted to its familiar name. A bizarre result of the twentieth-century expansion of the premises is that the River Ravensbourne now flows directly under the pub – though not, one hopes, through the cellar. This photograph, taken in 1897, when William Lomas was the landlord, also shows the Lower Mill (see p. 44).

There were once many allotments in Lewisham. These ones became the site of Romborough Way and the houses in Campshill Road in the early 1920s. The view is towards the High Street from the footpath which used to run between The Retreat (now Campshill Place) and Longbridge Road (now Campshill Road). The cul-de-sac on the right was Park Street, now Legge Street, which was built in the late 1860s. For the reverse view in the 1920s see *I 34*.

A garden party at the Lee Working Men's Club in the early 1920s. The club acquired this house, No. 115 Lee Road, in 1920. No doubt the pleasure of owning such a fine property was enhanced by the opportunities for annoying the members of the Lee Green Constitutional (formerly Conservative) Club, which had long been established at No. 119 – in a distinctly smaller house. The allotments beyond the garden are now the site of the Christian Science Church, and the cul-de-sac section of Meadowcourt Road.

Bandstands, which once adorned most parks, are not the least of the architectural losses of our ugly age. This handsome example in Hilly Fields, which stood some hundred yards north of Brockley County School, was a platform for free popular entertainment from the 1890s until it was demolished in the 1950s.

The forces which turned Southend from a village into a stretch of bland suburbia are plain to see in this bank holiday scene, c. 1920. The view is towards the Lower Mill pond, which had lately become a boating lake (see p. 44), with Beckenham Lane, now Beckenham Hill Road, on the left. Just out of picture on the right is The Green Man (see I 61), about to be rebuilt for the entertainment of all these visitors. They had mostly come by trams, the arrival of which in 1914 had been a turning point in Southend's history.

The natural curiosity about distant places and people is now amply satisfied by television documentaries, if not by personal travel. In Victorian and Edwardian times it was expressed in the form of enthusiastic patronage of lectures and lantern slides, and above all of raree-shows and museums. There were several of the latter in Lewisham. Next to his house at No. 38 Amersham Grove, Deptford, a master mariner called Archibald Taylor built a museum in 1890 to house the exotic souvenirs of a life of travel. At the Marquis of Granby at New Cross there was a presumably similar display in the early years of this century. Frederick Horniman's collection at Forest Hill (see *I* 124) was of the same species, but grown to a gigantic size. Crucially, Horniman was rich enough to build a museum for his treasures so large and grand that their permanent preservation was assured. This postcard shows the South Hall of the present Horniman's Museum in its early days. The hall is now largely devoted to African, Asian and American artefacts.

Another view of the New Cross Empire, with the Broadway Theatre in the distance (see *I* 121 and 122). The archway in the right foreground is the entrance to the Zion Baptist chapel. Beyond it is the courtyard of the Addey and Stanhope School (see p. 14). The actor who sent this card noted that his company rehearsed *The Cowboy and the Girl* at the Empire and played it at the Broadway.

The Central Hall, so called because it stood at the periphery of the shopping centre, at the corner of Sangley Road and Bromley Road, was built by James Watt, the proprietor of the Catford Picture Palace (see *I* 126) in 1912–13. This postcard was sent out in 1927 (when the adjoining row of shops, the Central Parade, was brand new) to advertise the cinema's latest silent attractions: *Beau Geste* with Ronald Colman, and the First World War epic *The Big Parade*. The Central Hall is now the Catford Cannon, the only cinema, out of so many, surviving in the borough.

Changed Utterly

. . . I securely stray
Where winding alleys lead the doubtful way,
The silent court, and op'ning square explore,
And long perplexing lanes untrod before.

Wells Park Road, now largely demolished, *c.* 1922.

Old Deptford was a town of two parts, the riverside village by St Nicholas's church and the Green, and the settlement on the Dover Road around the bridge and the Broadway. Deptford Church Street, now a windswept bypass lined by blocks of flats, was the link between these two parts, and thus an important road when the High Street was little more than a track known as Butt Lane. Church Street became the shopping centre, while Butt Lane developed mostly as a residential street. But the small shops of Church Street, predominant in the eighteenth century, could not be adapted to the expansive requirements of Victorian retailing so readily as the large houses of Butt Lane, which therefore became the High Street while Church Street slowly decayed. This photograph shows some of the seventeenth- and eighteenth-century houses on the west side of Church Street in 1920. The view is southwards towards the railway viaduct, from opposite Bronze Street. The house with the oriel window (No. 147) was The Trinity Arms until 1914, when it became a Roman Catholic club. All of these buildings were cleared to make way for a block of flats called Bates House, but that has gone in its turn, and this area is now part of the open space around St Paul's church. Nearly all the old buildings of Church Street have been demolished – most in the 1960s – to produce the present desolation.

The view down Clifton Hill, now Clifton Rise, from the New Cross Road in the autumn of 1927. On the right is the New Cross Kinema (see *I* 127), which was then showing the First World War naval story *The Battles of Coronel and the Falkland Islands*. Almost all the houses seen here, built mostly in the 1850s and '60s, were swept away twenty years ago to create Fordham Park.

Lewisham Road, now another planners' and architects' wasteland, was formerly lined by excellent late Georgian and early Victorian houses. Nos. 109 to 121, seen here *c.* 1914, stood on the north side between Blackheath Rise and Morden Hill. The three nearer houses, known as Belmont Terrace, were built *c.* 1845, the two semi-detached pairs beyond (Sandfield Place) *c.* 1842. All were destroyed by bombing during the Second World War.

Wilmore Place, earlier known as Williams Buildings or Alley, lay off the south side of Loampit Vale, just west of the railway viaduct running up to Lewisham station. The sharp-eyed will be able to spot it, next to Horton's timber yard, in the aerial photograph on pp. 150 and 151. It was built at the beginning of the nineteenth century as part of the Fox Estate, the first large scale working class district of Lewisham. Here lived the servants, labourers, laundresses, firewood cutters, prostitutes, who looked after the needs of the growing middle class population of the town. This, and the two photographs opposite, may serve as representative examples of the hundreds of cottages hidden in courtyards and alleyways, which were once such a feature of Lewisham, but have now almost all disappeared. Wilmore Place was swept away in a slum clearance programme shortly after this picture was taken c. 1935. The Sundermead Estate now occupies the whole area.

Grove House, a large mansion which stood in the High Street where the entrance to the Lewisham Centre is today, was demolished *c.* 1836. Among the hundreds of houses built upon its gardens in the next few years were these two terraces. Romer Place was an alley leading off the High Street in the area now occupied by Littlewoods and British Home Stores. Nos 2 to 12 (above) were on the north side. Romer Place led into the original Engate Street, which lay considerably to the north of its modern successor. Nos 10 to 20 Engate Street (below) stood opposite the turning to Romer Place. Both terraces were the victims of a slum clearance programme, *c.* 1936; but this was only anticipating their fate, because the district was razed for the Lewisham Centre in the late 1960s.

The eastern side of Lewis Grove, originally the eastern side of Lewisham High Street, contained some old houses, some of which can be glimpsed on the right of this photograph. The one with the bow windows was the Greyhound beerhouse. All have now been replaced by modern shops in the dullest of styles. Ernest Arthur Dubois started business as a hatter at No. 3 Lewis Grove in 1883 and gradually expanded until his department store dominated the northern end of the street. He died in 1927, and the firm was bankrupt six years later. Madame Harrison's Parisian School of Dressmaking failed to flourish c. 1910.

This picturesque terrace in Lewisham High Street was called Exchequer Place because George Edmunds of Sion House (see p. 98), the owner c. 1800, was an official of the Exchequer Office of Pleas at Lincolns Inn. As the workhouse, now Lewisham Hospital, expanded northwards the houses were demolished (c. 1891), with the exception of the nearest, which was incorporated with the hospital, and still survives, greatly altered.

The Retreat, Hither Green, later known as Campshill Place, was built in the late 1820s on the site of an old orchard. The main developer was the Revd Thomas Timpson, a congregationalist, who was minister of the Union Chapel in Lewisham High Street. No. 17 (right) was one of the terrace built for him, and he lived in the tall whitewashed house in the photograph below. This early 1950s view also shows the ominous approach of the new flats on the Hether Grove Estate; the Campshill Place houses were to be replaced by more of the same in 1954.

In the eighteenth and nineteenth centuries Blackheath was an area of smart middle class housing, with the odd aristocratic or even royal mansion. Such districts need to squeeze in, unobtrusively, a few alleyways or mews for the necessary servants and workmen. Two such were Bath Place (above) and Paragon Place, both pictured in 1938, a year before they were demolished during Lewisham's slum clearance drive. Bath Place, hidden between Blackheath Grove, Montpelier Vale, and Wemyss Road, was a growth of the late eighteenth century. The photograph looks westwards towards the junction of Montpelier Vale and Tranquil Vale. Paragon Place, the mews behind Montpelier Row, developed in the 1790s. Some of the stables (later garages) retained a connection with the Montpelier Row houses, others were taken over by carriers and job masters, and some were converted into cottages. This view is northwards from about half-way up the road. Since the war Paragon Place has become the centre of a council estate.

Two views of Ladywell Road in 1897. The mid-eighteenth-century group above, known as Charles Place, which stood between the bottom of the old vicarage garden and Wearside Road, was pulled down in 1900. The shop used until recently as Olby's show-room occupies the site. The early nineteenth-century cottages below, at the corner of the modern Malyons Road, were part of Alma Place. They were demolished in the 1930s and lock-up garages now take their place. The house glimpsed on the extreme right is No. 74, also part of Alma Place. Nos 74, 76 and 78, with the adjoining Ladywell Tavern, are the only pre-1850 buildings surviving in the village of Ladywell.

Lee New Town (see *I* 50) in May 1953, just before the coronation. On the left is No. 26 St Margaret's Passage, part of a terrace built in the 1840s, and known at first as Royal Oak Place. Below are Nos 23 to 69 Fludyer (formerly Dacre) Street, which dated from *c.* 1830. All these properties went in the first great wave of post-war demolition in the area, *c.* 1955. The site of the St Margaret's Passage house is just south of the garden of the Dacre Arms; the open space in front of the flats numbered 22 to 68 Boone Street marks the position of most of the Fludyer Street terrace.

Most of the Victorian houses at the eastern end of Lee High Road have survived so far; but the ones on either side of Lee Park (seen here *c.* 1910) were all replaced by flats in the 1960s and '70s. The houses on the left, between Dacre Park and Lee Park, were called Essex Villas. Beyond were South Lodge, Suffolk Terrace, Park Villas, and Cambridge House, all built in the 1860s.

Burnt Ash Hill in the 1920s. This is a companion piece to my view of Catford Hill (see *I* 39), for it shows another quiet spot transformed into a crucial junction on the South Circular. On the left is the turning to Baring Road and St Mildred's Road, which has since been widened and straightened; and the trees and garden walls on the right were flattened in the late 1930s by the irresistible advance of Westhorne Avenue. The 1870s houses on the left have all been demolished, and their site is now part of the Newstead Road estate.

Looking up Westwood Hill from the entrance to Shenewood in May 1964, shortly before these and most of the other houses on the north side were swept away in an orgy of destruction. The two Campion Houses (see p. 131) were among the fallen; Longton Grove was nearly obliterated at the same time, and No. 8 Jews Walk, the house in the background on the right, was another loss. These Westwood Hill houses were built in the early 1850s. The nearer two – No. 30, known as Cleveland Villa or Enderby, and West Hill Lodge, No. 32 – were larger versions of the surviving mock-Tudor houses in Jews Walk and on the lower slopes of Westwood Hill. The site of the demolished houses was soon occupied by rows of flats, which turn their backs and a long blank wall to Westwood Hill, transforming it into a one-sided road.

The Purple of Commerce

And costers' carts and crowded grocers' shops
And Daniels' store, the local Selfridge's,
The Bon Marché . . .

Tower House, Lewisham High Street, *c.* 1935 (see p. 27).

The Perry Hill post office (see *I* 134) is put into context by this postcard, which shows the forecourt of the Perry Hill branch library (see *I* 116) behind the wagon, the entrance to Alfred Sykes's builders yard beyond, and, with the carriage outside, No. 16a Perry Hill, the house Mr Sykes built for himself *c.* 1880. Two of the pinnacles of St George's church are visible above the tree.

This strange building stood at the corner of Lee High Road and Brightfield Road, on part of the present Sainsbury's site. It was 'erected regardless of cost, in commemoration of the 1887 Jubilee' as the Jubilee Coffee Tavern, became the London and South Western (later the Midland) Bank *c.* 1906, and survived until the early 1950s, when the Midland moved to new premises – recently vacated – across the road.

'Neighbour Florist' looks like a fancy name, but in fact the man in the doorway was Edwin Neighbour, who ran this shop at No. 119a Deptford High Street for many years until his death *c.* 1926. It seems a small enough business, but the profits were sufficient to allow Mr Neighbour to live in Manor Road, Brockley, then a very respectable address. (See also p. 92.)

George Painter and Son established their greengrocery at No. 86 Rushey Green, immediately north of the Rising Sun, *c.* 1905. One or more further sons were later taken into the business, which expanded into No. 84, and flourished at least until the 1930s.

Frederick Ward ran his sweet shop and dairy at No. 2 Turner Road, Lee, later No. 71 Dacre Park, from *c.* 1897 until 1928. He is probably the man on the left. Like most of Lee New Town (see *I* 50) this shop has been demolished, but the houses in Kingswood Place, behind the wall on the right, are still standing. The photograph was taken in the spring of 1925, when the Blackheath Dramatic Club was performing Noel Coward's *The Young Idea* at the Blackheath Concert Halls. The Italian maid Maria was played by Millie Karlowa of The Hollies (see p. 106).

Robert Bowyer's dairy at No. 310 Lee High Road, *c.* 1918. On the right are Nos 1 to 13 Bankwell Road, built in 1908. The shop, which now deals in videos, is of the same date.

Royal Parade, Blackheath was built in 1861–2 as a right-angled development, of which only the part facing directly onto the heath retains the name. The section shown in this postcard is now Nos 37 to 49 Montpelier Vale. The date is *c.* 1903, when Burnside's bookshop was in exile at No. 4 Royal Parade (now No. 43 Montpelier Vale) while his old shop in Tranquil Vale was being rebuilt. On the left is the entrance to Tranquil Passage (see p. 132).

Springfield Avenue was the original name for these shops, now numbered 2 to 28 Rushey Green. They were built in the early 1880s on the garden of the late eighteenth-century house called Springfield, the childhood home of the entomologist Henry Stainton (see *I* 128). Part of the old house was converted into Nos 20 and 22, glimpsed on the left of this photograph which was taken *c.* 1903. The Misses Lewis at No. 6 sold art needlework. Albert Sunnuck of No. 8 was an oilman.

Devonshire House, No. 2 London Road, Forest Hill, seen here *c.* 1897, was built in the 1850s as part of a row called Havelock Terrace, and served for years as the local post office. Its career as one of Cullen's grocery chain was cut short in 1915, when it was decided to extend the tram lines from London Road into Devonshire Road, and this corner shop was demolished to make the curve less sharp.

This shop at the corner of Egmont Street and Brocklehurst Street will be familiar to many old Millwall fans as a landmark on the weary trudge back to New Cross Gate station. The photograph probably dates from 1920, when Horace Percy Hudson took over the business. These and the adjoining streets were built in the early 1870s on the grounds of the moated manor house called Hatcham Park.

Edward Charles Christmas founded his building business at No. 55 Dartmouth Road, Forest Hill, in 1888, and the firm remained on the site (although the shop was rebuilt) until the early 1970s, by which time they had become estate agents. The original shop, seen here *c.* 1897, was converted from one of a group of cottages built *c.* 1830 and known at first as Dartmouth Row.

William Thomas's junk shop at No. 121 Deptford High Street. One of the posters above shows that the photograph was taken in 1911, when the Festival of Empire was being staged at the Crystal Palace. On the left is Edwin Neighbour's flower shop (see p. 87).

Herbert Bindon's butchers shop at No. 80 Rushey Green, just north of the Rising Sun and George Painter's greengrocery (see p. 88). Bindon opened his shop in 1896. This photograph dates from *c.* 1930, when the business was taken over by John Best of No. 148 Rushey Green.

Rushey Green at its junction with Willow Walk in 1897. This is practically the reverse of the photograph on p. 18. Mrs Mary Ann Martin at No. 156 Rushey Green was a tobacconist. Brown, the fishmonger and poulterer, was at No. 152. Willow Walk is now Winslade Way, the entrance to the Catford shopping centre; so the plastic cat now fishes for pedestrians at the corner on the left of this view.

Murdoch's music shop at No. 138 Lewisham High Street in 1914. On the left is Avenue Road, later Romer Avenue and now the main arcade of the Lewisham Centre (see also *I* 130). The adjoining premises were the Sample Shop, Ellis Bros., who sold leather goods, and the Lotos and 'K' Boot Depot. On the far right is the former Wheeler's sweet shop (see *I* 32).

Manor Park Parade, Lee High Road was built c. 1895 on the garden of Lee Lodge (see *I* 47). This photograph shows Nos 1 to 4, *c.* 1910. No. 1 was a dairy for many years, and run at this time by Joseph Gatcombe. Mrs Janet Wood had her stationery and toy shop at No. 3, *c.* 1905 to 1925. The houses on the left, Nos 121 and 123 Lee High Road and No. 2 Belmont Park, were demolished to make way for Archbishop Coggan House.

Lonsdale and Bradey, Ko-Ko tailors, founded their branch at No. 58 Lewisham High Street in 1914, when this photograph was taken. The shop, the fifth south from Rennell Street, is seen at a much earlier date in the lower picture on p. 28. Rebuilt, it is now the Chelsea Building Society.

Bellingham Terrace was the name for these shops in Bromley Road, on either side of Bellingham Road, when they were built c. 1910. The postcard shows them a year or two later. David Frederick Nevill ran the motor and cycle works at No 21 and 22 Bellingham Terrace, now Nos 243 and 245 Bromley Road, from 1910 to 1913. It is now part of the London Tyre Warehouse premises.

Bromley Road at its junction with Downham Way, c. 1930. These shops, little changed today, had just been built for the benefit of the tenants of the Downham Estate built in the 1920s, who had previously been forced to travel to Catford or Bromley for their shopping. The LCC offered very favourable leases to attract big names like United Dairies to this new frontier.

Desirable Residences

And here the haberdasher with his wife,
His ledger closed, sits down to close his life.

Hurst Lodge, Lee High Road in 1887 (see p. 99).

Sion House in Lewisham High Street began as an inn called The George (probably not connected at all with the present one of that name) and was rebuilt in this form in 1732. It became a private house fifty years later, and from 1838 to 1859 was the home of the Wood family (see *I* 10). This photograph was taken by Henry Wood in the late 1850s. Sion House was demolished in 1972, and the site is now part of the car park beside Lewisham library.

Hurst Lodge in Lee High Road, the
exterior of which is shown on p. 97,
dated from 1819. It formed a pair with
Lee Lodge (see *I* 47) which was built by
the same landowner on the same field.
These photographs of the hall and the
drawing room were taken in 1887 for
the Kersey family, the occupants from
1880 to 1924. Thereafter the house
became the offices of the factory which
spread over the gardens. The flats
known as Lee Court were built on the
High Road frontage *c.* 1936, hiding
Hurst Lodge from view; but it survived
until 1983, when the whole site was
cleared for the creation of Halley
Gardens.

Ravensbourne Park, Catford was a quality estate of the 1820s and '30s, and a number of houses of that period survive. Development in the Crescent began a little later, with Ravensbourne Park House (above) built in 1843. The photograph shows members of the Hollebone family, wine merchants, who lived there from 1861 to 1890. The house was demolished *c.* 1909, and Polsted Road built across its site. The view of Ravensbourne Park Crescent below shows, on the left, the lane which led to Ravensbourne Park House and Blythe Hill and, on the right, Summerfield, a house built in the early 1850s and demolished in the mid-1920s. Nos 43 to 49 Ravensbourne Park Crescent now take its place.

Firhill Lodge, Southend Lane was probably built *c.* 1815, in what was then a very isolated part of Sydenham, on the right bank of the Pool River. It had grounds of about thirteen acres, which now form a significant portion of the Bellingham Estate (see p. 155). The family most closely associated with the house was that of Samuel Pegg, an iron merchant, there from 1848 to 1879. The house was bought by the LCC in 1921 and demolished four years later. Firhill Road now crosses the site. The extravagant piece of late Victorian mock-Tudor glimpsed on the right in this photograph of *c.* 1900 was Southend House, the only other property in this part of Southend Lane before the building of the Bellingham Estate. The dog was called, very likely, Patch.

Brindley House, at the corner of Lewisham Way and Shardeloes Road, was built in 1860 for Edward Humphreys, a marine engineer. It was subsequently known as Bryn Towy, the name still to be seen on the front, and then became a school called Knightsville College. For most of this century it has been a hall of residence for Goldsmiths' College under the name of Surrey House.

The Maples stood at the southern end of Lewisham High Street, at the corner of George Lane, from the 1790s until 1890. The most eminent resident was Sir John Aird MP, civil engineer, who built the Aswan Dam.

John Penn (1805–1878), the son of a Greenwich millwright, rose to fame and fortune as one of the leading pioneers of the marine steam engine. He employed thousands of men at his factories in Deptford and Greenwich (see *I* 107 and 151), where the engines for many of the Royal Navy's first ironclads were made. In 1856 he bought Lee Grove, which he renamed The Cedars (see *I* 41) and largely rebuilt.

West Lodge was built at the corner of Eliot Vale and Love (now Heath) Lane, Blackheath in 1880–81. Its site was at the north-eastern extremity of the Cedars estate, where in John Penn's time there had been only a genuine gatekeeper's cottage. West Lodge is now divided into several dwellings, and numbered as part of The Close.

This mirror photograph, taken in the music room, gives some idea of the grandeur of The Orchard, the last major Blackheath house to have been demolished. It was built *c.* 1780 on a piece of ground enclosed from the heath, and before long became a convenient home for the widows and unmarried daughters of the Earls of Dartmouth. Later occupants of interest were George Frean, the biscuit baron, and Sir Assheton Pownall, MP for East Lewisham. In the 1890s, houses – in Eliot Vale, Orchard Drive, and The Orchard – were built over most of the garden, but the old house survived until wantonly destroyed in 1964. The flats called Lyncourt were the worthless replacement.

Cedar Lodge, formerly Dell Lodge (above) was built at the corner of Lewisham and Morden Hills in the late 1790s, and greatly enlarged in 1806, for John Green, an art collector. The entrance was in Lewisham Hill, but the main front faced Morden Hill, from which this view was taken. West Bank (below) stood at the northern corner of Lewisham Hill and Blackheath Rise. The house can also be glimpsed above the roof of Cedar Lodge. West Bank was built in 1863 for Samuel Smiles (1812–1904), the author of *Self Help*, who had previously lived in Granville Park. The family remained until 1874. When these photographs were taken, *c*. 1930, both houses had become nurses' home for St John's Hospital; both were demolished after bomb damage in the war.

The hall and dining room of The Hollies, Lewisham (see p. 115 and *I* 47) in 1910. Otto Karlowa, a German merchant (though some of his domestic arrangements have more of a Russian flavour) moved here with his English wife in the early 1880s, and the family remained until *c.* 1926. Although the house has been boarded up for several years, it is still standing.

Ravensbourne Terrace, an attractive group of houses built *c*. 1830, stood between the Sydney Arms and the Lewisham Silk Mills, in the part of Morden Hill south of Lewisham Road. Like other small but respectable houses in Lewisham they were popular with retired or half-pay officers of the army and navy. This was Ravensbourne Cottage, No. 26 Morden Hill, which stood nearest to the Sydney Arms. With the rest of the terrace, it was badly damaged by a flying bomb in 1944 and demolished in the following year. Nos 5 and 6 Rosewood Gardens now occupy the site.

Westwood House, Sydenham, one of the old homes of the Lawrie family, was largely rebuilt between 1879 and 1881 to the designs of John Loughborough Pearson (1817–1897). His client was Henry Littleton, the chairman of Novello and Company, the music publishers; many famous artists, including Liszt, performed in the great music room. In this century Westwood House became the Passmore Edwards orphanage for the children of teachers. It was demolished in 1952 and the estate called Sheenewood took its place.

In most of the lavish developments which mushroomed around the Crystal Palace mock-Tudor was the preferred architectural option. The exception was the Lawrie Estate, laid out in the mid-1850s, where Charles Barry junior set the tone for a gracious late flowering of his father's Italianate style. A good example was Willoughby House, later known as St Aubyn's and, finally, as The Haven, No. 42 Crystal Palace Park Road, which was built c. 1860 and demolished in the 1970s. The photograph shows it c. 1930, when it was the Motor and Cycle Trades Children's Home.

Oaklands, Forest Hill was built at the top of Honor Oak Park in 1856. It formed a pair with the long-demolished Observatory House, the home of Edwin Clark (see p. 126), which stood opposite. Oaklands remained a private house until the First World War. Afterwards it became the Sacred Heart School, in connection with the adjoining convent, which lies just over the borough boundary in Southwark.

Charles Bayer, a German, made a fortune in corsets before the bottom fell out of that market. He bought a large house in Honor Oak Road called Tewkesbury Lodge (demolished 1930), and on either side built fine homes for his eldest son and daughter. Havelock House, the daughter's, is now incorporated into the police complex. This is Hamilton House, No. 36, built for Herbert Charles Bayer *c.* 1900. It is now the Eurocentre.

Bromley Hill House, sometimes known as Warren House, is doubly unusual in Lewisham as a substantial country mansion (with over a hundred acres of grounds at its peak), and as one which still survives. It was built in 1767 or shortly after for William Slade of the Middle Temple on the site of a smaller house called Windmill Farm. Its great days began in the 1790s, when the estate was bought by Charles Long, afterwards Lord Farnborough of Bromley Hill (1761–1838). He was the colleague and close friend of William Pitt, and our greatest prime minister was a regular visitor to the house, which he liked to use for important meetings. Lord Farnborough, who was artistic advisor to George IV and William IV, devoted forty years to the enlargement and embellishment of Bromley Hill, which as seen in this photograph (c. 1900) was very much his creation. His nephew and heir Samuel Long kept up the house in grand style, rarely employing less than twenty indoor servants to look after just himself and his wife. The break up began in 1883, when Samuel Cawston bought the estate and started to build on the beautiful grounds. It was his son Colonel Cawston who turned the house into an hotel in 1919. It did not prosper immediately, though, and in 1927 the colonel was tried (and acquitted) on a charge of attempting to burn it down and claim the insurance. Luckily, little damage was done, and Bromley Hill House still stands as the Bromley Court Hotel. The new use has involved alterations, but much remains the same. The drawing room, for example, is still quite recognizable from a watercolour painted in 1816.

Leisured Pursuits

Will ye pitch some white pavilion, and lustily even the odds,
With nets and hoops and mallets, with rackets and bats and rods?

Watching cricket at Grove Park, *c.* 1910.

Two of the many cricket clubs which flourished in Lewisham in the late nineteenth century, when there was still plenty of space available for pitches. The Granville Cricket Club, seen above *c.* 1893, was one of the smartest. Its ground was in Manor Lane, Lee, until the western end of Holme Lacey Road and the Chiltonian biscuit factory (see p. 59) were built over it in the 1920s. The Bromley Road Cricket Club (below, in 1899) was rather less exclusive. This was the Lee Bromley Road, now called Baring Road, and the club's ground was at Horn Park – probably the one acquired by the Old Colfeians in 1902.

The Private Banks cricket ground at Catford (see *I* 77), almost certainly during a county match, *c.* 1905. Kent usually played here a couple of times a season during that classic era. The houses in the background were in Berlin Road, now called Canadian Avenue (see p. 146), which was laid out *c.* 1879. The five uniform houses, Nos 7 to 15, most of which survive, were built in the early 1880s, and originally called Alnwick (far left), Dresden House, Caradon, Harrowins, and Endon. Winthorpe, on the right (No. 17), was added *c.* 1899, as were most of the other houses in the road. The tower in the background, on the left, belonged to St Laurence's church (see pp. 156 and 157), which was built in 1886 and pulled down in 1968.

A busy cricketing scene in Sydenham Recreation Ground, now known as Mayow Park, during the great game's Edwardian high summer. The park had opened in 1878, just in time to save a number of clubs whose traditional grounds were being swamped by the ever rising tide of house building in Sydenham and Forest Hill. Among the teams that played here were Albion, Comet, Holmwood, Victoria, and the Sydenham Early Closing Association.

That famous ritual, the cricket tea, being enjoyed at a ground somewhere in the Lewisham area, probably in Lee or Blackheath. Among the players were members of the Bowditch family of Holly Lodge (see pp. 119 and 121).

What was the compulsion which drove the members of St Augustine's church, Grove Park (see I 70) so frequently into fancy dress? This is the St Augustine's Cricket Club posed near Sydenham Cottages, Marvels Lane in the 1920s, with Grove Park Hospital in the background.

Croquet was not a common game in the comparatively cramped gardens of suburbia, but the wide lawn of The Hollies (see p. 106) was well adapted to it. The photograph was taken in September 1910. This pleasant spot is now covered by the 'Budget Beds' warehouse in Molesworth Street.

'Simian Schoolboys meet the Catford Hill Boaters' might have been Hollywood's title for the top picture, which unites two of my favourite sets of characters (see pp. 40 and 41, and *I* 24 to 26.) The original 1898 view is captioned 'Above Catford Bridge'. For the photograph below see the opposite page.

Edwardian middle class life rarely looks more attractive than in these scenes on the Ravensbourne at Catford Hill. The two canoeists in the lower photograph opposite were Albert Wells and his sister. The picture above, entitled 'Conversation Piece', continues the story begun on *I* 24. The dashing George Wells has now lured Cissie Duffin into his canoe, but along comes the interloper, Jack Stanford, to spoil their idyll. The Wells family lived at Clovelly, No. 33 Catford Hill, the Stanfords at Deepdene, No. 43. Albert and George Wells and Jack Stanford appear in the group photograph on *I* 25. Today the river runs behind shops at this point, and flood prevention measures have confined it within high concrete banks; but a faint hint of the atmosphere can still be savoured in the pleasant park which follows the banks of the Ravensbourne and Pool upstream towards Sydenham.

Morriss William Brown and his wife Emily taking tea in the conservatory of Isleham, No. 17 The Glebe, on the borders of Lee and Blackheath, *c.* 1910. Brown, a draper, lived here *c.* 1888 to 1914. He was evidently a man who deprecated waste, for he had previously lived at No. 33 Bennett Park, which was then also called Isleham. The Glebe is a fairly well preserved piece of Victoriana, but Isleham is sadly one of the losses. It was bombed during the Second World War, and one of the blocks of flats on the Prendergast Road Estate now occupies the site. For another view of the house see p. 120.

Scenes in the garden of Holly Lodge, Wisteria Road, Lewisham, *c*. 1910. This was a detached house on the east side, opposite the pairs shown on p. 145. There is now a small block of flats there, insultingly flaunting the same name; and this pretty garden is a car park. The three little maids fresh from a ladies' seminary, above, and *en travestie* below, were the daughters of Charles Edward Bowditch, who lived at Holly Lodge *c*. 1900 to 1912. For other photographs of this happy family see pp. 114 and 121.

Two tennis parties from the classic age of the drawing room comedy. The one above took place *c.* 1920 in the garden of Amblecote Lodge, now No. 122 Amblecote Road, Grove Park. The house was built in 1913 for Frederick Arthur Wilson, the man standing, and the family lived there until *c.* 1934. The scene below is Isleham, The Glebe, the date *c.* 1910, and the people Morriss Brown and his family. The conservatory is the one in which Mr and Mrs Brown are seen at tea on p. 118.

Members of the Bowditch family of Holly Lodge (see p. 119) enjoying a game of tennis in the Manor House Gardens, Lee, a few years after they were opened to the public in 1902. The players are seen (above) near the southern entrance to the park, with Taunton Road in the background. This is still a tennis area, though now the courts are hard, and enclosed by a wire fence. They also have nets, which was apparently not the case in these early days, as a member of the family is clearly carrying one home in the picture below. The party has just crossed the Quaggy footbridge, and is passing the eastern end of the pond.

In the tennis-crazy Edwardian suburbs a court in the garden was a distinct status symbol, sometimes only achieved by the narrowest of margins. The one above was in the garden of Inversnaid, No. 5 Chinbrook Road, Grove Park, the home of the Dandridge family. One has heard of local rules for trees on cricket grounds, but never for tennis courts. The future of the greenhouse seems precarious.

Badminton in the garden of Norfolk Villa, No. 95 Lee Road, during the 1930s. The houses on the right are in Manor Way. Norfolk Villa was the home from 1934 until his death in 1968 of L.A.J. Baker, the Blackheath antiquary. Note the blurred image of the falling shuttlecock.

SECTION TEN
All the Amenities

> *... the time*
> *Is conscious of her want; through England's bounds,*
> *In rival haste, the wished-for Temples rise!*

All Saints' church, Blackheath, *c.* 1900.

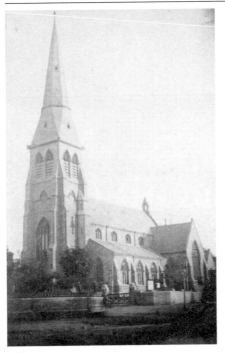

Brockley Congregational church (left), seen here shortly after it was completed in 1861, was sometimes known as St David's, in honour of David Williams Wire, Lord Mayor of London, who lived nearby at Stone House and largely financed the building. It was demolished in 1968 and replaced by the pastiche Victorian houses numbered 158a, b, and c, Lewisham Way. Deptford Congregational church in the High Street (below) was founded on this site in 1702 and rebuilt in 1772–3. The photograph shows this second chapel shortly before it was demolished in its turn in 1862. Since then a couple more chapels have come and gone, and the site is now occupied by the Deptford Job Centre. What happened to the graveyard? A good question.

St Mary's church, Lewisham, seen here from Ladywell Bridge, *c.* 1860, in a photograph probably by Henry Wood. It shows the church as rebuilt in the 1770s, before the addition of the large chancel in 1881–2. Next to the tower can be seen the back of Church House (see *I* 64), and on the right edge of the picture is the weather-boarded rear of Sion House (see p. 98). In the background appears the roof of the newly built Lewisham Park Villa, which is now, as No. 78, the only survivor of the first generation of Lewisham Park houses. The unembanked Ravensbourne was then quite a wide river. To its left was a piece of glebe land called Church Field, treated at this time as an unofficial park, but subsequently taken as the site for the old swimming baths, the church hall, and the St Mary's Institute.

Honor Oak Park was a development of the late 1850s and early '60s on land belonging to the Earl of St Germans, and was originally known as St Germans Road or Semaphore Hill. Development began from the Honor Oak Road end, more or less along the line of an old footpath. The builder was Edwin Clark, who provided the site – one of the best in south London – for St Augustine's church, built in 1872-3. It could hardly fail to be dramatic, but it cannot be said that the architect, William Oakley, did much to improve on nature. In his defence he would probably have alleged that he designed the church with a spire, which could never be afforded. The perfunctory tower was substituted in 1888. The house on the left in this 1890s view is Ashdale, built *c.* 1865 and now divided into flats and known as No. 103. If the old lady opposite Ashdale could suddenly have been transported back seventy years she would not have been walking, but wading up to her neck in the Croydon Canal, which ran across the line later taken by Honor Oak Park at exactly this point. Ashdale had a fragment of the old canal as an ornamental feature in its garden.

The architectural history of Lewisham is neatly illustrated by this area of Rushey Green. Catford Methodist church was built in 1896 on part of the site of the large villa called Rosenthal (see p. 10). The church and the adjoining houses, one of them notorious in the 1950s as 'Haircut' Cole's pet shop, were demolished in their turn in 1966–7 to make way for Capital/Rosenthal House, a large filing cabinet.

St Dunstan's church, Bellingham Green, was built in 1924–25 to the designs of Sir Charles Nicholson, as a chapel-of-ease to St John's, Southend. This photograph of the choir entering the church was probably taken on 21 November 1925, when the dedication service was conducted by the Bishop of Southwark.

The Tonbridge line, which was opened in 1865, seen *c.* 1900 from the bridge between Courthill Road and Morley Road. At the bottom of Courthill Road, on the left, is Lewisham Congregational church. On the other corner can be glimpsed Yew Tree Villa, which was replaced in 1911 by the Gild Hall (see *I* 123). In the same year houses called Bolton Terrace were built on the allotments between the road and the railway.

The Florence Road bridge over the North Kent line of the South Eastern Railway, which was opened in 1849. The view is south-eastwards towards St John's: the signal box beyond the bridge no longer exists. Florence Road, a development of the late 1840s, is fairly well preserved, but Nos 57 and 59, seen on the left, do not survive.

In Edwardian times, just as today, New Cross was the meeting place for many varieties of transport, several of which appear in this busy scene at New Cross Gate. Horses, though, were on their last legs. From 1909 to 1917 No. 182 New Cross Road, the premises of Charles Ranford in this view, was to house the Electric Empire cinema. The building still survives, as does the White Hart.

Two open-topped electric trams in New Cross Road, *c.* 1908. Behind them are Fairlawn Mansions, built in 1906, the South East London Synagogue, opened in 1904 (and recently replaced by a Jehovah's Witness church), and beside it the entrance to the New Cross tram depot, for which see *I* 87.

The Sydenham High School, one of the excellent foundations of the Girls' Public Day School Company, or Trust, had its first home from 1887 to 1934 at Longton Hall (above, *c.* 1910), at the junction of Westwood Hill, Taylor's Lane, and Longton Grove. It had been built *c.* 1854 as the Longton Hotel, a hydropathic establishment, and was demolished in the 1960s. In 1934 the school moved directly across Westwood Hill to its present home at Horner Grange (below, *c.* 1898), a luxurious house of the late 1870s which had declined after the First World War into a maternity home and residential hotel.

The spacious Victorian houses of Upper Sydenham became increasingly difficult to let during this century, and as a prelude to demolition or conversion into flats, many of them had periods as orphanages or schools. Campion House, No. 82 Westwood Hill, was built *c.* 1860, in the heady early days of the Crystal Palace, and originally occupied by a banker. The Misses Geake and Bishop (one of whom is presumably to be seen on the left in this picture of the garden front) opened it as a 'high class girls' school' with 'finishing classes and kindergarten' *c.* 1900. In 1914 Miss Geake moved the establishment two doors down to No. 78, and continued to finish the young ladies of Sydenham there for many years. Hardened local historians will not be surprised to learn that the school retained its old name in the new premises. Like most of the houses on the north side of Westwood Hill (see p. 84) Nos 78 and 82 were demolished *c.* 1964.

Tranquil Passage, Blackheath in 1952, showing on the right Tranquil Hall which, for a small building, has served the community in a surprising number of ways. It originated in 1851 as an infants' school, the gift of the Legge family, the lords of the manor, and continued as the All Saints' church school until 1939. It then had a spell as a venue for meetings and the like – the Blackheath Art Society were holding an exhibition there when this photograph was taken – before becoming the Blackheath Village Library in 1962. This moved to its present home in Blackheath Grove in 1988, and since then the old hall has been used as an office.

St Mary's National Schools, which stand opposite the parish church in Lewisham High Street, were built in 1833 during the struggle for the hearts and minds of the people between the Anglicans and the Nonconformists in the wake of the first Reform Act. (The rival establishments of the dissenters were called the British Schools.) The original building is on the right in this view of *c*. 1917, and on the left is the extension of 1860. Amazingly, and delightfully, the school remains the same, except for some minor additions at the rear.

Plassy Road (later Rushey Green) School was built *c*. 1880 as one of the School Board for London's assertive fortresses of popular education. Like Plassy Road (see p. 146) it suffered in recent decades from planners' blight, having been marooned on an island in the South Circular. The children were moved to safer premises in the 1970s, and after some years of use as a teachers' centre and for adult education the building was closed *c*. 1985.

Deptford Town Hall in New Cross Road (see *I* 114 and 155) nearing completion in 1905. The architects were the firm of Lanchester, Stewart and Rickards, specialists in this field, and the builder H.L. Holloway of Deptford Church Street.

Lewisham Town Hall in Catford Road was built as the headquarters of the Lewisham Board of Works in 1874–5 and enlarged in 1900 – the section beyond the small gable to the left – for use by the new borough council. This photograph shows it decorated for the coronation of George V in June 1911. The building was demolished in 1968 and the civic suite put in its place. Note the Whitehall Memorial (see p. 19) on the right.

A number of patients and nurses were injured when the Park (now Hither Green) Hospital was bombed on the night of 11 September 1940. This was the scene of destruction revealed on the following day.

Blackheath's 'South Bank' in Lee Road was the creation of the latter-day Renaissance man William Webster (1856–1910). His was the organizing genius behind the building of the Concert Halls (on the right in this photograph) in 1895, and the Conservatoire of Music and School of Art, hidden behind the conservatoire, in 1896. All three were designed by the partnership of James Edmeston and Edward Gabriel. (See also *I 159*.)

Three lost public buildings, seen here in the 1940s. St Margaret's House in Old Road, Lee (left) was built *c.* 1879 and sold by the church in 1961. By then the parish rooms (centre) had also been disposed of (see *I 94*). They were built by the local architect George Barnes Williams, who died in 1887. As a memorial his widow paid for the Working Men's Institute, later the Lee Centre, in Aislibie Road (right), built in 1889–91 to a design by their son Thomas Barnes. In recent times it came under the papier-mâché aegis of Goldsmiths' College and was closed last year.

New Cross Fire Station (above), at the corner of Queen's Road and Waller Road, was
built in 1894 on the site of Hatcham Manor Farm (see I 11). The Lee Green Fire Station
(below) has stood at the corner of Eltham Road and Meadowcourt Road since 1906. It
replaced the one in Lee High Road (see I 36). The old ivy-covered house in the centre of
the photograph, No. 7 Eltham Road, formerly Radway Cottage, still survives in a rather
dilapidated state. It was named, after his home town, by a crony of Charles Lamb.

There is no smarter set of almshouses than Morden College, which lies just off the south-eastern corner of Blackheath. It was founded by Sir John Morden in 1695 on an outlying part of his Wricklemarsh (now the Cator) estate, and was originally intended for the relief of 'decayed Turkey merchants', the Levant trade having been the source of Sir John's wealth. Membership is now less exclusive, and perhaps even poulterers may be eligible. The college is attributed to Sir Christopher Wren, but the library (seen above), one of a series of extensions in the north-eastern angle, was added only in 1860–1, to the designs of Philip Hardwick. It is known as the Kelsall Library, after Charles Kelsall, a former resident of Greenwich, who left the college his books and two thousand pounds to pay for the building.

Byways

Through Groves, so call'd as being void of trees,
(Like lucus *from no light); through prospects named*
Mount Pleasant, as containing nought to please,
Nor much to climb . . .

Courthill Road from the corner of Ryecroft Road, *c.* 1910 (see p. 144).

Prince Street, Deptford, at the corner of Peter Street (left) in the 1870s. Peter Street was a cul-de-sac leading to a minor gate of the royal dockyard. It was swept away, and this side of Prince Street largely rebuilt *c.* 1881, when Dacca Street was created.

Rural Place seems here almost to justify its name; but in fact it was a turning off Queen's Road, only a tram's creak from New Cross Gate. The houses were built in 1856, and called Prospect Place because they looked out over the fields of the Haberdashers' Estate. The name did not remain appropriate for long, and was changed to the equally inaccurate 'Rural' in 1937. The terrace was demolished *c.* 1974, eight years after this photograph was taken, and Swallows Close on the Somerville Road Estate now occupies the site.

St James's church was built in 1854, and St James's, the cul-de-sac by which it is approached from New Cross Road, was soon lined with smart semi-detached houses. The ones on the right (all now displaced by the church school) were built in the 1850s and '60s; those on the left in the 1860s and '70s. Of these only the ones at the far end (Nos. 17 to 31) survive. The old church has now become part of Goldsmiths' College, and a new one has been built to the right of it.

The junction of Avignon Road, Brockley with Aspinall Road (left) and Dundalk Road, *c*. 1910. On the brow of the hill in the distance is the church of St Catherine, Hatcham (see *I* 67). Walter Mason ran his grocery shop at No. 45 Aspinall Road from *c*. 1905, when it was built, until 1924.

Belmont Grove seen from Belmont Hill nearly a century ago. It was created in the late 1850s, on the edge of John Penn's Cedars estate (see p. 103). Most of that original development survives, but Gothic House, where Ernest Dowson was born in 1867, has long been supplanted by the flats called Dowson Court. The pretty lodge was demolished in 1948.

Church Terrace, Lee, which still provides a dignified setting for St Margaret's church, was built on land belonging to Thomas Brandram of Lee Grove, later The Cedars. The houses on the south side came first, in 1845–46. Of those on the north, seen here, the two nearer pairs, Nos 16 to 13, were added in 1849, and Nos 12 to 9 in 1855–56. Only Nos 9 and 10 in the distance, have been demolished.

Algernon Road seen from Vicar's Hill in 1886. A few years later this view was blocked as Embleton and Ermine Roads were formed across the grassy foreground, and the west side of Algernon Road was gradually developed. These houses on the east side (No. 153, on the left, to No. 187) had just been completed in 1886, and many were still unoccupied. Like most of Algernon Road and the neighbouring streets they were the work of the eminent local builder Samuel Jerrard. Behind the houses can be glimpsed the railway line from Lewisham to Ladywell and the winding course of the Ravensbourne River. Beyond that is Lewisham High Street, with the Congregational church prominent; and in the distance are the square villas in Lingards Road and Morley Road. This view should be compared with those of Lewisham cricket ground (see I 76) which occupied this area until the 1880s.

Like Dr Watson, Courthill Road, though dull in itself, has been a source of inspiration: witness this evocative photograph, and those on pages 128 and 139. This one of *c.* 1910 looks north-east towards the spire of Lewisham Congregational (now United Reformed) church in the High Street. It is the reverse of the view on p. 139, which was apparently taken on the same occasion from outside the school seen here on the left. The photographer was perhaps a teetotaller, as he has carefully omitted the Sir David Brewster on the right of this picture and on the left of the other. The house with the tall gable, No. 2 Ryecroft Road, was known as Tudor Lodge until it became a school under the name of Athena House (*c.* 1900 to 1911). It still survives, as do most of the houses in both photographs, though the area no longer looks so solidly prosperous.

Wisteria Road, Lewisham, looking south from the right-angled bend, *c.* 1905. These houses on the west side were known as Cambridge Villas. The two pairs with the attractive porches were built *c.* 1870, the rest *c.* 1876–7. All those in this view have been replaced by the developments known as Wright Close, etc.

Slaithwaite Road in the mid-1870s, with Hilly Fields in the distance. Building had begun *c.* 1863, and by this date had proceeded as far as No. 23 on the north side (right), and to No. 14 on the south. The dirt track on the left was Lingards Road, in which only Nos 6, 7 and 8, at the other end, had then been built. The site of Slaithwaite, Morley, and Lingards Roads belonged to Lord Dartmouth, and had previously been part of the garden of The Limes (see *I* 42).

Nos 19 to 43 Berlin Road were built *c.* 1899, five or six years before this photograph was taken. During the First World War the Canadian Forestry Corps was based at Catford, and in 1918, on the day after Armistice Day, Berlin Road was renamed Canadian Avenue in its honour. The corps band paraded 'an unflattering effigy of the Kaiser' through the streets before the Canadians personally tore down the old street signs. (See also p. 113.)

Plassy Road, seen here *c.* 1910, has been one of the victims of geography. It was built in the 1880s, and remained a quiet backwater until its strategic position marked it out for ruin as part of the Catford one-way system. So this is another in my series of South Circular transformation scenes (compare p. 83 and *I* 39). On the left is the wall of Plassy Road Board School (see p. 133).

The Firs, a seventeenth-century house on the west side of Old Road, Lee, was knocked down in 1892–3, and Lochaber, Abernethy, Rembrandt and Murillo Roads laid out over the fine gardens. This is Lochaber Road, *c.* 1900. The houses were mostly built in 1893–4, by E.J. Taylor. On the far side of Lee High Road is Brandram Road, running up past the leafy grounds of the Merchant Taylors' almshouses to St Margaret's church.

Recreation Road viewed from Sydenham Recreation Ground, now Mayow Park (see p. 114). These two houses on the south side, Nos 2 and 4, which were built *c.* 1900, survive not greatly altered; but the larger one beyond, No. 42, Silverdale, was bombed during the Second World War and has been replaced by a block of flats. The postcard was published *c.* 1905.

Torridon Road, Catford, *c.* 1910, when a sunny afternoon had brought out a cloud of pinafores to greet Perkins and Son's photographer. His view was northwards from near the southern end, with the turning to Ardoch Road on the left. The cluster of Scottish names indicates that this was part of the St Germans Estate, built from the late 1890s by the great developer Cameron Corbett MP and now usually known by this name. The conscientiousness of his work means that the phrase 'a Corbett house' is still one to conjure with among estate agents; but the quality of life for his tenants was somewhat reduced by his equally conscientious refusal to allow any pubs in this wide tract of Catford and Hither Green. Torridon Road, this part of which was built *c.* 1905, features examples of the smallest version of the Corbett house. When new this type could be purchased, freehold, for about £350.

SECTION TWELVE

Overview

As when a man, that sails in a balloon,
Downlooking sees the solid shining ground
Stream from beneath him in the broad blue noon . . .

The view from Hilly Fields over parts of Ladywell, Lewisham and Hither Green, *c.* 1930.

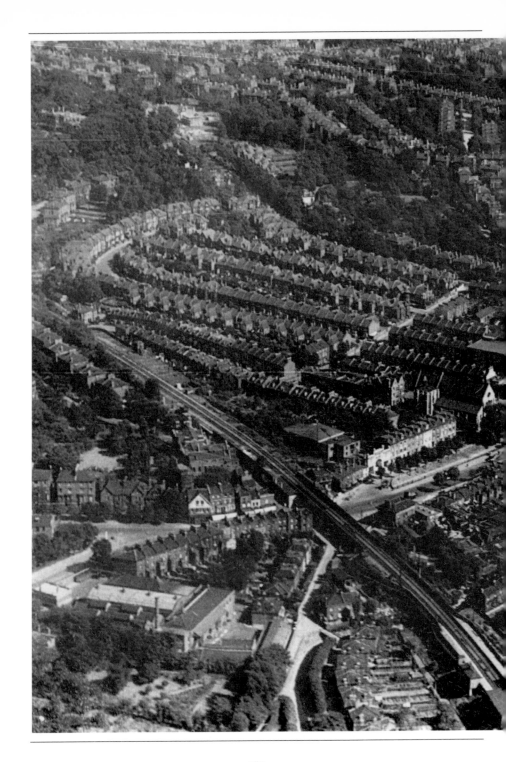

Blackheath Vale and the Hare and Billet Pond, *c*. 1924. The Vale was an old sandpit, in which houses began to be built at the end of the eighteenth century. The pond was a smaller pit with a different fate. Below it is Grote's Place, an earlier encroachment upon the heath, and the fine houses of Eliot Place, with their gardens still intact.

Previous pages: This panoramic view of Lewisham (*c*. 1924) shows so much of the borough, from Hither Green, top right, to Lee, top left, that I would need a volume to describe it adequately. Much of the interest is at the bottom, where the central feature is Lewisham station. To the left is the Anchor Brewery in Lewisham Road, which was built in 1817, and only quite recently replaced by Tesco's supermarket. It is curious to note that not one of the many buildings contained within the curve of the railway viaduct in the bottom right hand corner is still standing. They included the business premises of two men commemorated by street names in the area. The building behind the tall chimney of the Chislehurst Laundry had been the headquarters of Samuel Jerrard, the builder; and the complex next to the railway bridge on the other side of Loampit Vale was Benjamin Horton's timber yard. The large building just below the railway line on the extreme right was Lewisham Bridge Mill (see *I* 102). The area above it, between the railway and the High Street, has also been largely swept away to make room for the Lewisham Centre. Three buildings of interest which were destroyed during the Second World War were the Lewisham Methodist church (with the spire) in Albion Way, the King's Hall cinema by the railway bridge at the top of the High Street (see *I* 125), and on the other side of the bridge, at the foot of Granville Park, the old All Saints' Boys' Orphanage, which later became an annexe to Colfe's Grammar School.

The central portion of Lewisham High Street from Limes Grove to Ladywell Road, with parts of Lee and Hither Green beyond, c. 1924. The photograph is neatly divided by the Tonbridge line (see p. 128), running up to Hither Green station, top right. In the top left corner is Manor Lane, with the unmistakable curve of Manor Park below, and, nearer to the railway line, Leahurst Road School. Further down the left side are Morley and Slaithwaite Roads (see p. 145) converging close to the High Street. The part of the High Street left of the railway line had been a residential area of some quality, with houses ranging in date from c. 1700 (Camden House, next to the bridge on the near side) to the 1850s (Limes Villas on the far side), but by this time almost all had become shops. On the right side of the railway, the open area at the bottom is the Wearside Road council depot. Points of interest in the High Street include the Gild Hall, next to the bridge on the far side, with Brooklands House opposite, at the corner of Whitburn Road (see I 123 and 21). Lewisham Congregational church is prominent on the southern corner of Courthill Road. Nearly opposite are Sainsbury's shop and depository next to the Castle; and at the corner of Ladywell Road is the large garden of Lewisham Vicarage, now Ladywell House. On the right edge of the photograph is Lewisham's first council estate (Romborough Way, etc.); and above it, in complete contrast, Campshill House in Hither Green Lane, a fine mansion a century old at this time, and with its well-wooded garden still intact. It was replaced by the Hether Grove Estate in the late 1940s. The square open space between Campshill House and Hither Green station was the drill ground belonging to the Ennersdale Road barracks of the Lewisham Gunners.

Hither Green from the air, *c.* 1924. The road running from the bottom centre, where it crosses Torridon Road, to the top right is Hither Green Lane. The group of large buildings to the left of it is, of course, The Park or Hither Green Hospital (see p. 135). Starting from the bottom left, I will circle the hospital in a clockwise direction, pointing out features of interest. The turnings off the left side of Hither Green Lane between Torridon Road and the hospital are Benin Street and Woodlands Street. The latter led to the spacious early Victorian development called The Woodlands. Two of the dozen houses which composed it (all now demolished) can be seen at the end of Woodlands Street. Above the hospital is Mountsfield Park (see *I* 128), and beyond it Davenport Road and George Lane running down to Rushey Green. At the top of the picture is Lewisham Park, and top right is St Swithun's Church, with Beacon Road School directly below. The building with the Dutch gable at the turn of Hither Green Lane, just at the top right corner of the hospital, was the Park Cinema, now a shop. The industrial building on the right, with the chimney, began life *c.* 1897 as the builder's yard of Bassett and Son, contractors for the Corbett Estate (see p. 148). In 1924 it belonged to Kelvin, Bottomley and Baird, nautical instrument makers. Today International House and the Social Security office occupy the site, at the corner of Duncrievie Road.

The view from Downham Fields towards the Crystal Palace, *c.* 1930. In the foreground is the Downham Estate, newly built by the LCC, with Downham Way on the left and Churchdown on the right. The large open space in the middle distance on the left is Beckenham Place Park.

Bellingham, the LCC's other big estate in Lewisham, was built just before Downham, in the early 1920s. This photograph of *c.* 1924 shows it approaching completion. The view is from the east, or Bromley Road side, and shows Randlesdown Road running from the bottom right across Bellingham Green to meet Firhill Road at top centre. The latter was named after the then recently demolished Firhill Lodge, for which see p. 101.

Bromley Road runs from the right hand side to the top of this view, taken *c*. 1924. In the bottom left corner are Knapmill Road on the new Bellingham Estate, the railway from Catford to Bellingham, and a stretch of the River Ravensbourne. The photograph is dominated by three large buildings. Bottom right is part of Bromley Road bus garage, opened in 1914. Above it and to the left is the Gleniffer Laundry, which was established *c*. 1910. This building, now occupied by Initial Services, is still used for the same kind of work, but James Robertson's Golden Shred preserve factory (above and to the left again), which was built *c*. 1900, no longer has any connection with jam. It is now the premises of Franklin Mint, makers of commemorative medals and the like.

Previous pages: In this excellent aerial view of Catford, *c*. 1924, most of the features of detailed interest appear in the bottom half. I will point them out from left to right. On the left edge Brownhill Road branches off Rushey Green, and on the corner are the Lewisham Hippodrome and the Queen's Hall cinema (see p. 19). The white-striped roof to the right belonged to part of Timpson's garage (see *I* 88 and 89); and just beyond is Plassy Road School (see p. 133). The centre is dominated by the town hall, and the old St Laurence's church opposite, the former now replaced by the civic suite and the latter by Laurence House. The tower of the church partly obscures the Central Hall cinema (see p. 72), which was about to be joined by the Central Parade. The white building to the right of the cinema, in Bromley Road, was Sangley Lodge, one of the great houses of Catford, which was demolished in 1933–34. This is the only image of it I have seen. In the bottom right hand corner, in the large garden, is a house which still survives: Elmwood, the Catford Conservative Club. It began as a farmhouse built in 1735 (the double-roofed section), but was greatly extended *c*. 1870, before becoming the Conservative club in the mid 1880s. The farmer from 1785 until the 1840s was James Thomas: Thomas Lane is named after him. Opposite Elmwood is a corner of the Private Banks cricket ground (see *I* 77). At the top of the photograph, development on the Forster Estate had proceeded only as far as Arran Road, except for the partially built Bellingham Road in the distance.

It is striking how open this fairly central part of Lewisham was as recently as 1924. The main feature of the photograph is the Bermondsey Workhouse, later Ladywell Lodge, for which see p. 53. The water tower on the left is one of the few fragments which still survive. In the bottom left corner we see how slowly the development of the Bridge House Farm Estate (see p. 39) had proceeded. Here, twenty five years after work began at the Phoebeth Road end, is the building site where Amyruth and Henryson Roads now meet Chudleigh Road. The railway bottom right is the one from Crofton Park to Catford. Its curve encloses part of the Southern Railway Athletic Club ground. The line of trees snaking from middle right to top left marks the course of the Ravensbourne, which is crossed midway by the railway from Ladywell to Catford Bridge. The open space on both sides of the track on the right, and beyond it on the left, is of course Ladywell Fields, then known as Ladywell Recreation Ground – a less attractive name for what was then a far more attractive park. At the top of the picture are Lewisham High Street and Rushey Green, from Colfe's almshouses on the left to Prendergast School on the right. The main feature here is the present hospital (left of centre), which was then still the Lewisham Workhouse. At first glance, who would have thought that this almost rural-looking scene would turn out to include two of those grim bastilles?

Acknowledgements

Most of the photographs in this volume are from the collection of the Lewisham Local History Centre, and I am grateful to the London Borough of Lewisham for permission to reproduce them here. A number of others are from the Martin Collection at the Greenwich Local History Library, Woodlands, Mycenae Road, London SE3. It is a great pleasure to thank Mr Julian Watson, the librarian, for bringing these treasures to my attention, and Mr Neil Rhind, the Martin trustee, for allowing me to use them. The copyright photographs in question are the one on p. 18, both on pp. 39 and 81, and the lower photographs on pp. 31, 68, 93 and 145. My sincere thanks also to Mr W.J. Seaman for giving me access to his fine collection of Sydenham postcards.

For the captions I have drawn heavily on Neil Rhind's standard histories, *Blackheath Village and Environs* (volumes 1 and 2, 1976 and 1983) and *The Heath* (1987), and on Ken George's account of early Lewisham cinemas, *Two Sixpennies, Please* (1987). Both authors have been very generous in answering my supplementary questions.

Lastly, my thanks to those who have sent me corrections to *Lewisham and Deptford in Old Photographs*. I hope soon to have an opportunity for incorporating them, when that work is reprinted.